Blessed God's Way

"A Blessing of Marriage, Faith and Love"

Blue Kendria

Copyright © 2025 by Blue Kendria Berry

All rights reserved.

No part of this publication may be reproduced in whole or in part, or stored in a retrieval system, or transmitted in any form or by any means, electronic, mechanical, photocopying, recording, or otherwise, without written permission and consent of the publisher, except brief quotes used in reviews.

Scripture quotations are taken from the World English Bible (WEB) and are used by permission (CC0). The World English Bible is in the public domain. For more information, visit https://worldenglish.bible.

This book is a work of fiction. Names, characters, places, and incidents either are products of the author's imagination or are used fictitiously. Any resemblance to actual events or locales or persons living or dead is entirely coincidental.

Blessed God's Way - *"A Blessing of Marriage, Faith and Love"*

(2nd Book in the God's Way Series)

Printed in the United States of America

First Edition, 2025

PAPERBACK ISBN: 979-8-3492-6055-1

HARDBACK ISBN: 979-8-3492-6057-5

EBOOK ISBN: 979-8-3492-6056-8

Red Pen Edits and Consulting

www.redpeneditsllc.com

Thankful to God for His unfailing love and incredible ability to work through me and the continued faithfulness to complete this series of God's Way. Without Him, this journey would not have been possible.

Table of Contents

CHAPTER 1 1

CHAPTER 2 7

CHAPTER 3 17

CHAPTER 4 23

CHAPTER 5 31

CHAPTER 6 37

CHAPTER 7 43

CHAPTER 8 53

CHAPTER 9 61

CHAPTER 10 65

CHAPTER 11 71

CHAPTER 12 77

CHAPTER 13 81

CHAPTER 14 87

CHAPTER 15 91

CHAPTER 16 99

ABOUT THE AUTHOR 103

CHAPTER 1

As the newly married couple, Troy and Love, made their way toward the airport, the soft glow of the moonlight cast a serene shimmer over the road ahead, their hands tightly intertwined. The rhythmic hum of the car blended with their quiet conversation and laughter as they reminisced about their wedding just hours before. Every detail felt like a dream: the vows, their love, the love of their family and friends, the joy that radiated through the night.

Even though it was July, the evening air was refreshingly cool, a gentle breeze drifting through the open window. The temperature was perfect, neither too warm nor too chilly, just another subtle blessing that made the early morning hours feel even more magical. Love leaned her head on Troy's shoulder, sighing happily as they continued their journey, hearts full of love and anticipation for what the honeymoon was to bring.

"Babe, we're married!" Love exclaimed.

Troy glanced at her, his heart swelling with love. "It feels like a dream come true and I know it's just the beginning of a blessed life together. We have so much ahead of us, Love. So many moments to look forward to."

Love smiled, her eyes shining with joy. "I'm just so very happy, Troy. Thankful for you, for us, for everything we've built and are building together."

Troy squeezed her hand, looking ahead at the road that led to a lifetime of blessings. "I'll always thank God for bringing us together. You're the answer to every prayer I've ever prayed."

The car arrived at the airport, and they stepped out, their excitement growing as they walked toward the terminal. The world around them seemed to slow down, everything and everyone fading into the background except for the two of them. The blessing of starting this new chapter of their life was palpable, and Love felt an overwhelming sense of peace, knowing that no matter what challenges lay ahead, they would face them together.

They got checked in and then found a quiet corner in the terminal to sit and wait for their flight. Troy pulled out a small box from his bag and handed it to Love with a smile.

"What's this?" she asked, raising an eyebrow.

"A little something to signify our lifelong journey together," Troy said, his voice soft.

Love carefully opened the box, revealing a delicate silver Pandora bracelet with two intertwined rings as charms. "Troy, it's beautiful and it will go right on with my "God's Perfect Timing Bracelet," she whispered, her fingers tracing the design.

He smiled warmly. "It's just another symbol of our bond, how it is unbreakable, and how it is forever. I want you to have something to remind you that no matter where life takes us, you'll always have my heart."

Love's eyes filled with emotion as she clasped the bracelet around her wrist. "I'll wear it always," she promised.

They awaited their flight, scheduled to depart at 3 a.m. Troy had thoughtfully upgraded their tickets to business class, ensuring extra comfort for the long journey. The perks included cozy seats, in-flight entertainment, and a delightful breakfast.

Once they boarded, Troy and Love settled into their seats, snuggling close as they prepared for takeoff. Love had always carried a quiet fear of flying, but sitting beside Troy and feeling his steady presence and the reassuring way he held her hand brought her an unexpected sense of calm.

Sensing her nervousness, Troy leaned in, pressing a gentle kiss to her forehead before closing his eyes. Without hesitation, he began to pray softly, his voice a steady anchor amid the hum of the cabin.

"Lord, thank You for Your mercy, your grace, and your peace. We ask for Your protection over this flight, that You keep the plane in perfect order and guide us safely to our destination. Thank You for Your unwavering love and faithfulness. We trust in You completely. With sincere hearts, we say, Amen." "Amen," Love said in unison.

As he finished, a ripple of agreement moved through the cabin. From across the business class section, several passengers quietly responded, "Amen."

Troy and Love exchanged surprised glances before smiling warmly. In that moment, they were reminded once again that faith has a way of bringing people together, even in the most unexpected places.

"Thank you babe", Love said quietly. "No thanks needed. I will alway pray over you, over us. I could feel that you are a little nervous," Troy responded. Love smiled and squeezed his hand.

The seven-and-a-half-hour flight turned out to be a delight. They watched movies, shared laughter and conversation between them and others on the flight, and savored their breakfast, making the experience feel more like a mini adventure than a long-haul trip.

Around 5:30 a.m., Troy peeked out of the window shade and grinned. He could not keep the sight to himself. "Love," he whispered softly, but she remained still, nestled against his shoulder with her eyes closed.

"Love," he repeated, this time gently rubbing her shoulder.

She stirred, her voice groggy but sweet. "Yes, babe?"

"Look," Troy said, his smile stretching wide. "You've got to see this."

Love blinked her eyes open and turned toward the window as Troy slowly lifted the shade. Her breath caught as she took in the sight. The horizon glowed with the soft hues of dawn, and the sun's golden rays painted the clouds in brilliant shades of orange, yellow, and pink.

"Wow, Troy," she whispered, awe evident in her voice. "This is breathtaking. I thought I'd be terrified even to look, but this... This is proof of God's artistry. No one can tell me He doesn't exist. It's absolutely amazing to see."

"Babe, can you take some pictures for us?" she asked, her eyes still glued to the mesmerizing view. "You're closer to the window."

"Of course, my love," Troy replied. He reached for his phone and began snapping photos from different angles, capturing the beauty of the sunrise from above the clouds.

The couple remained in awe, watching as the sun fully emerged over the horizon, casting a breathtaking golden glow across the endless sky. The soft hues of orange and pink melted into brilliant blue, painting a masterpiece only God could create. It was a sight so serene, so divine, that neither of them spoke; they simply sat in the moment, letting the beauty sink into their souls.

As the plane soared forward, Love nestled closer into Troy, feeling the steady rise and fall of his breath. She closed her eyes for a moment, her heart overflowing with gratitude not just for this journey, but for the man beside her, for the love they shared, and for the presence of God in every step of their lives. Troy pressed a gentle kiss to her lips, as if sensing the depth of her emotions, and in that quiet, sacred space above the clouds, they rested, ready for whatever lay ahead.

They decided to leave the shade open, enjoying the view as the plane glided through the sky. Around 10 a.m., a stewardess asked everyone to turn off their electronics and prepare for the descent. Business-class passengers stirred, putting away their belongings.

Troy powered down his phone, which he had used to capture memories for their honeymoon scrapbook. Love hadn't taken hers out at all, too engrossed in soaking up the moment. After securing their electronics and folding up their tray tables, they heard the captain announce over the intercom that the descent was beginning.

They both turned their attention to the window, watching the ground come closer. The descent was smooth at first, but then the plane hit an air pocket, causing a sudden jolt. Love nearly jumped out of her seat, instinctively grabbing Troy's arm and burying her face in his shirt, her eyes squeezed shut.

When another air pocket caused the plane to drop slightly, she let out a small yelp and clutched Troy tighter. Troy chuckled softly, wrapping his free arm around her.

"Don't laugh, babe," Love mumbled, her voice muffled against his arm. "Are we going to crash?"

He rubbed her arm gently, his tone soothing. "No, my love. It's just air pockets in the clouds. Completely normal."

"Well, I don't like the air pockets," she replied, shivering slightly.

Troy noticed her trembling and shifted to hold her more securely. "Aww, baby, you're really nervous," he said tenderly. "It's okay, I've got you."

Love tilted her head up, her eyes shimmering with unshed tears. "You promise?" she asked, her voice tinged with vulnerability.

"I promise," Troy said, his gaze steady and full of reassurance. "I'm going to hold you tight until we land."

And he did just that. Troy kept his arms wrapped around her, whispering calming words until the plane finally touched down. The sound of the tires hitting the pavement was like music to Love's ears.

She lifted her head, her face streaked with slightly smudged mascara from her nervous tears. Troy smiled and handed her a face wipe and a small mirror.

"I will always take care of you, babe," he said softly.

She took the wipe and mirror, her heart swelling with gratitude. "Thank you," she whispered before leaning in to give him a long, heartfelt kiss.

She cleaned her face, catching her reflection in the mirror. A smile spread across her lips as she thought about how happy and incredibly blessed she was to have such an amazing caring man by her side. Once ready, she tucked the mirror and face wipe into her pocket and reached for her crossbody bag. Troy grabbed the other carry-ons with ease, and together they exited the plane.

CHAPTER 2

France Day 1

As they stepped into the bustling airport, the sheer energy of the place hit them. It was alive with movement passengers rushing to and fro, announcements echoing overhead, and a symphony of languages blending in the air. Love couldn't help but marvel at the chaos.

When they reached the doors leading outside, something caught her eye, a sign with their names on it, held up by a chauffeur standing next to a sleek black limousine parked next to the sidewalk. She paused, her brows furrowing slightly in confusion. Troy grabbed her hand and stepped outside onto the sidewalk in the windy weather.

"Umm, babe?" Love said, glancing up at Troy, who was slightly in front of her.

"Yes, my love?" he replied, as he looked down with a knowing grin spreading across his face.

Before she could ask her question, the driver, a man with a thick accent and a warm smile, approached them. "Troy? Love?"

"Yes, that's us," Troy confirmed.

"Excellent!" the driver said enthusiastically as he shook Troy's hand. "Bonjour! Welcome to France."

Love's jaw dropped, her eyes wide with astonishment. "France?" she whispered, spinning to face Troy. She realized she never looked around, just holding on to her amazing husband following his lead.

Troy chuckled at her expression. "Baby, I added some surprises to our honeymoon. Would you like to leave?" he teased, raising a playful eyebrow.

"SERIOUSLY! You brought me to France?!" No I don't want to leave, she exclaimed, practically bouncing on her toes with excitement.

The driver chuckled at her enthusiasm and stepped forward to open the door to the limo. "Bienvenue à Paris," he said with a flourish.

Love turned to Troy, her eyes brimming with happy tears. "I can't believe this," she said, her voice trembling with emotion.

Troy leaned in and kissed her. "This is just the beginning of our honeymoon, just wait and see."

Hand in hand, they climbed into the limo, ready to embark on the next chapter of their unforgettable honeymoon adventure.

As the limo pulled away from the airport, Love couldn't contain her excitement. She gazed out the window, taking in the sights of Paris as they passed: bustling streets, charming cafés, and historic architecture bathed in the morning light.

"Troy," she said, turning to him, her voice tinged with wonder, "I've dreamed of coming to Paris, but I never thought I would."

Troy reached for her hand, intertwining their fingers. "I told you, Love, nothing is too good for my wife. This is just one of the many dreams we're going to make come true together."

Love squeezed his hand, her heart full. "You're amazing. I don't know how I got so lucky."

Troy smiled, his eyes softening. "It's not luck, baby. It's all God's plan."

The limo slowed as it approached their initial destination. The driver turned and spoke. "We are here," he said, his voice carrying a touch of pride.

Love leaned forward, her breath catching as she saw where they had arrived. Standing before them was the iconic Eiffel Tower, its iron lattice shimmering in the golden light of the morning sun. A picnic set up awaited them on the nearby Champ de Mars, complete with a blanket, pillows, and an elegant basket filled with treats.

"Oh my goodness," Love whispered, her hand covering her mouth.

Troy chuckled and opened the door, stepping out first before extending his hand to help her. "Come on, Mrs. Hayes. Let's make this moment unforgettable."

She took his hand, stepping onto the lush green grass. "This is... perfect," she said, her voice trembling with emotion.

Troy led her to the picnic setup, where the driver had already begun unpacking non-alcoholic champagne and pastries. They sat together, the Eiffel Tower towering above them and the sounds of Paris waking up in the background.

As they shared croissants and toasted with champagne, Troy reached into his pocket and pulled out a small box.

"Love," he began, his voice serious yet filled with tenderness, "I wanted to give you this. They are a reminder of how much you mean to me and how everyday with you is a blessing."

He opened the box to reveal three beautiful diamond charms: a cross, a heart, and an airplane. He gently added the charms to the pandora bracelet he gave her at the airport.

Love gasped, her eyes brimming with tears again. "Troy... they're beautiful."

Holding her wrist he explained. "Each charm represents something special: our faith, our love, and the adventures we will share."

She leaned forward, kissing him deeply. "I love you so much, Troy."

"I love you too, Love," he replied, holding her close.

After savoring their last bites of flaky croissants and sipping the final drops of champagne, Love leaned back against Troy's chest, letting out a contented sigh.

"I don't think life gets better than this," she said, her voice dreamy as she gazed up at the Eiffel Tower.

Troy chuckled softly, brushing a loc from her face. "Oh, it does, Love. This is just the start. Wait until you see what else I've planned."

She turned to him, eyes sparkling with curiosity. "You're already spoiling me, you know that?"

"Absolutely," he said with a grin, standing up and offering her a hand. "But you deserve every bit of it."

She took his hand, and he helped her to her feet. The driver approached, carefully gathering the remnants of their picnic and loading everything into the limo with efficiency. As the driver placed the basket in the trunk, Troy called out to him with a warm smile.

"Excuse me," Troy said, stepping closer. "I just realized I didn't get your name. What should we call you?"

The driver straightened and replied with a polite nod, "Sam, sir. My name is Sam."

"Thank you, Sam," Troy said. "I have one more favor to ask would you mind taking a few pictures of us in front of the Eiffel Tower?"

Sam's face brightened. "Of course not, sir. I'd be happy to."

Troy handed Sam his phone, and he turned to Love, offering his hand. "Come on, babe. Let's capture this moment."

They posed in front of the iconic landmark, first standing side by side, then with Troy wrapping his arm around her waist. Love playfully leaned into him, laughing, and they even stole a kiss for one of the shots.

Sam snapped several photos, patiently adjusting angles to make sure the Eiffel Tower was perfectly framed behind them. After a few minutes, Troy walked over to retrieve his phone.

"Thank you so much, Sam," Troy said, shaking his hand.

"My pleasure, sir," Sam replied with a polite smile.

Troy and Love glanced through the photos, exchanging happy looks, before heading back to the car. Sam opened the door for them, and as they settled in, Love leaned her head against Troy's shoulder.

"Those pictures are perfect," she murmured. "Thank you for thinking of it."

Troy kissed her forehead. "Anything for you, Love. Moments like this deserve to be remembered."

As the limo pulled away, they stole one last glance at the Eiffel Tower, their hearts full and their memories captured forever. Once on the way the driver spoke with a smile. "Your hotel is just a short drive away. You will love it, it's one of Paris' finest."

Love glanced at Troy; her curiosity piqued again. "Troy, what kind of hotel did you book?"

He smirked, leaning back in his seat. "You'll see."

A few minutes later, the limo slowed and pulled up to an elegant building with wrought-iron balconies adorned with fresh flowers. A golden sign above the entrance read *Hôtel Lumière Royale.*

Love's jaw dropped. "Troy... this place looks like a palace!"

He grinned, stepping out first and reaching back to help her. "Only the best for my queen."

As they entered the hotel, the opulent lobby greeted them with marble floors, crystal chandeliers, and a grand staircase that spiraled upward. A concierge in a tailored suit approached them with a warm smile after shortly speaking with Sam, the driver.

"Mr. and Mrs. Hayes, I am Charles, welcome to Hôtel Lumière Royale," he said. "We have your suite ready. If you follow me, I'll show you to your room."

Love clung to Troy's arm as they followed the concierge to the private elevator. Her excitement grew with every floor they ascended. Finally, they stopped at the top, and Charles opened the double doors to their Penthouse suite. After they stepped inside Chales shut the door and left.

The room was breathtaking: floor-to-ceiling windows offered a panoramic view of the Eiffel Tower, while the suite itself was decorated with plush furnishings, gold accents, and a vase of fresh roses on the dining table.

Love walked in, spinning around slowly to take it all in. "Troy... this is beyond anything I could've imagined."

Troy placed their carry-on bags near the entrance and walked up behind her, wrapping his arms around her waist. "I wanted this to be unforgettable for you—for us. Do you like it?"

"Like it?" she whispered, turning in his arms. "I love it. I love you."

He leaned down, kissing her softly. "And I love you."

They spent the next hour exploring their suite, marveling at the luxurious touches and indulging in the welcome tray of macarons and non-alcoholic champagne that had been left for them.

As Love stepped onto the balcony to take in the view of the Eiffel Tower once more, Troy joined her, slipping his arm around her shoulders.

"This," she said, leaning into him, "is what dreams are made of."

"And this," he replied, kissing her lips softly, "is just the start."

There was a knock at the door. Troy walked over to answer it, with Love still standing on the balcony. When he opened the door, Sam, their driver; Charles, the concierge; and Vincent, the Executive Chef, stood waiting. "Sam. Charles. Nice to see you both again, Troy said warmly."

Sam and Charles nodded respectfully. "Sir, your bags have arrived from the airport, Charles said." Troy stepped to the side Charles and Sam rolled the luggage carrier into the suite, carefully unloading the suitcases and placing them neatly inside the closet.

Vincent stepped forward, handing Troy a few menus. "I am Vincent, your chef for the entirety of your stay. These are the room service menus," he explained, "as well as information on the restaurant downstairs, which serves lunch and dinner daily. We also have an exclusive executive menu for you as our VIP guests. My direct number is on the VIP menu. You can reach me or leave a message for any food request."

Having finished with the luggage, Sam and Charles came back and stood by Vincent at the door.

Charles then handed Troy a sleek card. "I will be your personal concierge for the duration of your stay," he said. "You can reach me at any time, day or night, on this number."

Sam also handed Troy his card. Anytime you need to go anywhere or if you need any information about the area you can reach me anytime.

"Thank you so much," Troy said with a nod and smile.

They all nodded simultaneously before beginning to turn away.

"Wait a moment," Troy called after them. He reached into his pocket, pulling out his wallet handing each of them $50.

Their faces warm in appreciation. "Merci, monsieur," they said in unison, nodding slightly before departing.

Troy shut the door and turned to find Love watching him, as she walked in from the Balcony doors, with a mix of awe and curiosity. "We get our own concierge, driver and executive chef?" she asked, her voice tinged with amazement. "Babe, did you arrange all this?"

Troy grinned. "I told them it was our honeymoon and that I wanted all the bells and whistles. Nothing but the best for my wife."

Her smile widened as she sat on the edge of the bed, she begin flipping through the menu. "Do you have anything planned for us tonight, or can we just stay in?" she asked.

Troy smiled, tucking a strand of hair behind Love's ear as he gazed into her eyes. "I figured we'd be tired after the flight, which is why I arranged for dinner to be brought to our suite. Tonight is all about relaxing."

Love's lips curled into a soft, contented smile. "Perfect," she murmured, her voice filled with warmth. "I just want time with you."

She reached for him, her fingers sliding gently along the back of his neck as she pulled him closer. Their lips met in a slow, lingering kiss—one filled with love, passion, and the unspoken promise of forever.

Troy deepened the kiss, his arms wrapping securely around her waist, drawing her even closer. The world outside their suite faded away, leaving only the steady rhythm of their hearts and the undeniable connection between them.

As their lips parted, Love rested her forehead against his, her hands still cradling his face. "I love you, Troy."

He brushed a thumb across her cheek, his gaze full of devotion. "I love you more, Love."

They decided to take a long bath together in their spa tub. Enjoying the relaxing hot tub jets to get relaxed after their travels. After getting out they put on their loungewear and headed to the loveseat. Troy stopped Love and grabbed both hands. He smiled at her. Lets pray, he began, "Lord thank you for your traveling mercies and your grace to make it here safe. Thank you for the ability for me to show my beautiful Love these amazing sights and blessings that you have bestowed on us. We surrender our plans and surrender to your will for us. Guide us and show us daily where you want us to go. Keep us safe in our travels. We will always give you praise! Forever and we say." Troy opened his eyes to see Love looking at him and smiling as they both said "Amen."

Just then, a soft knock at the door signaled the arrival of their early dinner. Troy stepped away briefly to let the hotel staff in, who quickly and quietly set up an intimate dining experience on the private balcony. The warm glow of candlelight flickered against the mid afternoon sky, casting a golden hue over the table set with an elegant spread of grilled seafood, fragrant rice, and fresh tropical fruits.

They took their seats, clinking glasses of chilled sparkling juice before diving into their meal. As they ate, they reminisced about their honeymoon so far, sharing laughter and quiet moments of adoration.

After dinner, they retreated inside, slipping into plush robes as they curled up together on the oversized chaise near the window. Love nestled into Troy's chest, his arms wrapped securely around her. The sound of the ocean waves in the distance mixed with the peaceful stillness of their suite, creating a sanctuary just for them.

"This is exactly what I needed," Love whispered, tracing gentle circles on his hand.

Troy pressed a kiss to the top of her head. "Me too, baby. Just you and me."

As exhaustion from the long journey settled in, they stayed wrapped in each other's embrace, the soft glow of the city lights painting a dreamy backdrop to their night.

CHAPTER 3

Day 2

The soft morning light streamed through the curtains, gently waking Love. She stretched lazily, her fingers brushing against Troy's arm as he lay beside her, still sound asleep. A smile spread across her face as she took in his peaceful expression. She carefully slipped out of bed, not wanting to wake him, and quietly walked over to the window. Pulling back the sheer curtain slightly, she gazed out at the breathtakingly gorgeous skyline.

A knock on the door broke her quiet reverie. She turned to see Troy stirring, his eyes fluttering open.

"Morning, babe," he said groggily, sitting up and rubbing his face.

"Morning," she replied with a soft smile. "There's someone at the door. Probably breakfast she said grabbing her robe off of the chaise lounge chair."

Troy nodded and got up, tossing on his robe before heading to the door. When he opened it, Charles stood there, accompanied by two staff members wheeling in a lavish breakfast spread on a cart.

"Good morning, Mr. and Mrs. Hayes," Charles greeted warmly. "Your breakfast as requested. We hope you enjoy it. If you need anything, please don't hesitate to call."

The staff set the table on the balcony, complete with fresh croissants, fruit, eggs, coffee, and juice. Once everything was in place, Charles and the staff gave a polite nod and left the suite.

Troy walked back into the room, smiling at Love. "Looks like we're starting the day in style."

She laughed, tying her robe tighter. "Every moment here feels like a dream."

They stepped onto the balcony, the crisp morning air carrying the aroma of freshly brewed coffee. As they ate, they planned their day.

"So, what's first on the agenda?" Love asked, sipping her coffee.

"I thought we'd start with a stroll along the Seine," Troy replied. "Then maybe check out the Louvre? Or is there something else you'd rather do?"

She shook her head, her eyes sparkling. "That sounds perfect. And maybe we can squeeze in a little shopping afterward?"

"Anything you want, my love," he said, leaning over to kiss her hand.

They finished their breakfast, showered, and dressed for their day. Love wore a chic sundress paired with a matching sweater and comfortable flats, while Troy opted for casual slacks and a button-down shirt. They left the suite hand in hand, ready to explore the city of love together.

Troy and Love stepped out into the lively streets of Paris, where the sounds of bustling cafes, cheerful chatter, and distant street performers filled the air. The Seine River sparkled under the morning sun as they walked hand in hand along its banks. Love paused frequently to admire the intricate details of the bridges and the picturesque boats gliding by.

"This city is so magical," Love said, squeezing Troy's hand. "I feel like I'm in one of those old romantic movies."

Troy smiled. "That's exactly what I wanted for us—a honeymoon straight out of a dream."

They stopped to watch an artist painting near Pont des Arts, the famous love lock bridge. The vibrant strokes on the canvas brought the river scene to life. Troy noticed Love's fascination and quietly arranged to purchase the painting. The artist handed it to him with a knowing smile.

"A little keepsake," Troy said, presenting the painting to Love. She gasped, her eyes filling with gratitude.

"Troy, it's perfect. Thank you."

They continued their stroll, making their way to the Louvre. Standing in the courtyard, Love gazed up at the iconic glass pyramid.

"I've seen pictures of this a million times, but seeing it in person is so different," she said in awe.

Troy wrapped an arm around her. "Let's go in and make some memories."

Inside, they wandered through halls adorned with timeless masterpieces. They marveled at the Mona Lisa, the Winged Victory of Samothrace, and countless other treasures. Love snapped pictures, and Troy captured candid shots of her admiring the art, her eyes wide with wonder.

After leaving the museum, they stopped at a charming bistro for lunch, where they decided to indulge in some different foods since they are in Paris, they decided to try escargot and coq au vin.

"You're really trying the escargot?" Troy teased as Love lifted a fork hesitantly.

"Don't make me second-guess myself," she laughed, taking a bite. Her eyes lit up. "Okay, this is actually delicious!"

Troy chuckled, "See? Paris is bringing out your adventurous side."

They spent the afternoon shopping along the Champs-Élysées, where Love picked out a few elegant pieces, and Troy surprised her with a custom perfume from a boutique.

They decided to return to the hotel around 4 p.m., they returned to the suite, tired but exhilarated.

"Today was incredible," Love said, sinking into the plush couch.

Troy joined her after finding a place on the writing desk to display the newly purchased painting, pulling her into his arms. "And tomorrow will be even better. We still have so much to see and do."

She leaned her head on his shoulder, her heart full. "I'm just so grateful for this time with you. Every moment feels like a blessing."

Troy kissed the top of her head. "Love, we have a lifetime of adventures ahead."

Love and Troy spent the afternoon unwinding, enjoying each other's company as soft music played in the background. They sat on the balcony, basking in the gentle breeze and the breathtaking view of the city, talking, people-watching and laughing as they sipped on cool drinks.

Troy had previously set his alarm for 6 p.m., so when his alarm went off, they decided it was time to get ready for dinner. Love slipped into a stunning evening dress, while Troy opted for a crisp button-up shirt and tailored slacks, both eager for a night of fine dining.

Once dressed, they made their way downstairs to the hotel's elegant restaurant. The ambiance was warm and inviting, with soft lighting, live piano music, and the aroma of gourmet dishes wafting through the air. A host greeted them warmly and led them to a cozy table for two by the window, offering a picturesque view of the city lights twinkling in the distance.

"This place is beautiful," Love said, her eyes scanning the room.

"Not as beautiful as you," Troy replied with a smile, reaching for her hand across the table.

They browsed the menu, marveling at the chef's creations, and placed their orders. As they waited for their meals, they talked about their favorite moments from the day, and how excited and happy they felt to be making these memories and experiencing so many adventures with one another.

When the food arrived, it exceeded their expectations. The food was perfectly seasoned and artfully plated. They savored every bite, pausing occasionally to exchange bites from each other's plates and share their delight in the flavors.

The evening was nothing short of magical as Love and Troy talked, laughed, and basked in each other's company. They decided to take their time, savoring the night as much as the delectable dinner they had just enjoyed.

Before heading back to their suite, they placed an order of cannoli's to enjoy while watching movies. The chef personally brought the order to their table, and they thanked him warmly for the thoughtful touch and exquisite presentation of their amazing 5-star 4 course meal.

With their sweet treat in hand, they made their way back to their room, walking hand in hand through the softly lit hallways. Once inside, Troy set the cannoli's on the small table near the loveseat while Love found a cozy blanket and dimmed the lights, creating the perfect ambiance for a relaxed evening.

"What should we watch?" Troy asked, scrolling through the options on the screen.

"Something light and funny," Love suggested, curling up on the couch and patting the spot beside her.

Troy selected a romantic comedy, and as the movie began, they shared the cannoli's, feeding each other bites and laughing at the scenes unfolding on the screen.

Halfway through the movie, Love rested her head on Troy's shoulder, feeling utterly content. "This is perfect," she murmured, her voice soft and filled with gratitude.

Troy kissed her forehead. "You deserve perfect, Love. Every day with you feels like a beautiful dream."

The night unfolded with warm embraces, shared laughter while enjoying their movie. By the time the credits rolled, Love was dozing lightly against Troy shoulder. He got up moving softly not to disturb her, picked her up and carried her to bed, tucking her in with care before joining her.

As they drifted off to sleep, the city lights twinkled beyond their window, a reminder of the incredible adventure they were living together. Tomorrow held the promise of new memories, but tonight was theirs a moment of love, peace, and gratitude for the blessing of one another.

CHAPTER 4

Day 3

The next morning, the soft glow of sunlight peeked through the sheer curtains of their suite. Troy stirred first, stretching lazily before turning to see Love still silently asleep, the sun showing off the beautiful natural glow of her caramel skin. He smiled, his heart swelling with gratitude.

Slipping out of bed quietly, Troy grabbed his robe and his laptop bag before stepping onto the balcony, closing the door gently behind him. The city stretched out before him in breathtaking beauty, with the Eiffel Tower standing tall in the distance, bathed in the soft golden light of morning. He inhaled deeply, letting the crisp air fill his lungs, and settled into a chair.

Bowing his head, Troy began to pray. He prayed for his new wife, Love, and for the beautiful marriage they were building together. His words were full of humility and gratitude as he asked God to always remain at the center of their union, to keep them grounded in Him, and to ensure they never placed themselves above one another or above God.

"Lord, give me the wisdom, guidance, and discernment to lead and cherish Love as Christ loved the church," he prayed, his voice trembling with emotion. "Help me to honor her, to submit to her as she submits to me, and to cherish her as the gift You've entrusted me with."

Tears began to roll down his face as he reflected on the depth of the love God had given him—a love he never thought he'd experience outside of Christ's unending grace. He thought back to the day their paths crossed, a day that had started with frustration. Troy had been ready to abandon his plans for lunch after dealing with a difficult contractor, but the Holy Spirit nudged him to visit his favorite spot instead. He smiled to himself, recalling how that small act of obedience changed the course of his life forever.

As he continued to pray, Troy thanked God for the smooth and natural rhythm of their relationship thus far and asked for strength and guidance for the days when disagreements or challenges might arise. "Lord, allow us to love one another even in the midst of disagreements, to communicate openly and with grace, and to grow together in You," he said.

After his prayer, Troy wiped his face, feeling refreshed and full of peace. He opened his bag and pulled out his Bible and notebook, placing them on the table beside him. Just as he sat them on the table, the soft sound of the balcony door sliding open caught his attention.

He smiled as he watched Love stepped out, her hair slightly tousled and her smile warm and soft. "Good morning, my handsome husband," she greeted, bending down to kiss his lips.

Troy smile matching hers. "Good morning, my beautiful wife," he replied, grabbing her, pulling her down on his lap and wrapping his arms around her. He leaned in for a longer, more passionate kiss, and Love melted into his embrace, her arms wrapping around him tightly.

When their kiss ended, they lingered in each other's arms, gazing into one another's eyes. Love began to blush. She looked away glancing out into the city, "The view is incredible, isn't it?"

"Yes, it is," Troy replied, his tone light and flirty, his eyes still locked on her. Love glanced over up at him, feeling the intensity of his gaze that hadn't shifted. She laughed softly, her cheeks warm and turning a delicate pink, but she didn't look away this time.

Troy leaned in, brushing his lips against hers in a tender kiss, slow and deliberate. When he pulled back, his eyes remained fixed on hers, filled with adoration. Love smiled, leaning in for yet another kiss.

"I love you with everything in me, babe," Love said, her voice soft yet steady, her words carrying the weight of her emotions.

Troy reached up, brushing one of her locs from her face, his touch gentle. "I love you more, mi amor," he whispered, his voice deep and heartfelt.

For a moment, there was nothing but them—lost in their own little world where time seemed to stand still. The bustling city beyond their balcony faded away, leaving only the soft sound of their breathing and the warmth of their shared embrace.

Suddenly, a loud car horn broke through the moment, startling Love back to reality. She jumped slightly, her eyes wide in surprise. Troy chuckled, pulling her closer. "It's okay, mi amor, I've got you," he said, his voice calm and reassuring as they both broke into laughter.

"My goodness, that kind of scared me," Love said with a giggle, her hand pressed to her chest as she tried to calm her racing heart. She stood, clutching her robe tighter around her as the chill of the morning air brushed against her skin.

Troy smiled, his eyes twinkling with amusement. "City sounds can be a little startling when you're caught up in such a perfect moment," he teased gently.

Love smiled big, her cheeks flushing. "Absolutely perfect moment"

"Every moment with you is perfect," he replied smoothly, his voice full of sincerity.

Love smiled, her heartwarming at his words. "Well, let's not let car horns ruin our perfect morning. How about we dive into that devotion?"

"Great idea," Troy said, gesturing to the chair beside her. "Have a seat, mi amor. Let's spend this time with God before the day takes us somewhere else."

"Yes, my love, well I came out here at the perfect time," Love said. "When I woke up and saw you weren't in bed, I looked out here and I saw you praying so I decided to take a moment to pray too. When I finished and saw you pulling out your Bible, I thought it would be nice to join you—if that's okay?"

Troy smiled warmly. "It's always okay, my love. I'd love for us to have devotion time together regularly." "Absolutely", Love replied with a smile.

He stood, pulled out the chair beside him and held it for her to sit. Love settled into her chair, and Troy joined her. As the city continued its lively hum in the background, they began their morning devotion, reading Scripture, and sharing reflections with moments of science to hear from God. As the sun climbed higher into the sky they enjoyed this moment growing their connection deeper not just with one another, but with God at the heart of it all. The love and faith they shared made the moment feel sacred; a beautiful reminder of the foundation they had built their marriage on. They reflected during the moment, understanding why it's said to be equally yoked, just to be able to share moments like this together.

They lingered on the balcony for a while, savoring the peaceful stillness of the morning, the distant hum of the city adding to the serene atmosphere. Eventually, they decided it was time to start their day. After refreshing showers, they chose to coordinate their outfits—matching denim with rich maroon accents, a subtle yet stylish statement of their unity.

Once dressed, they made their way downstairs to the hotel's cozy breakfast buffet. The spread was nothing short of impressive—an assortment of fresh pastries, artisanal cheeses, vibrant fruits, and an array of hot dishes. Love's plate quickly filled with buttery croissants and juicy berries, while Troy opted for a hearty omelet paired with a selection of savory meats. As they sat down to eat, they exchanged smiles, knowing another day of adventure awaited them.

As they ate, they talked about their plans for the day. Troy had arranged for a private tour of the Louvre Museum, followed by a leisurely afternoon exploring Montmartre, the charming arts district known for its cobblestone streets and quaint cafés.

By mid-morning, they were standing outside the Louvre, marveling at the iconic glass pyramid. Their private guide, a knowledgeable and passionate art historian, greeted them warmly and began the tour. Love's eyes sparkled as they walked through the galleries, marveling at masterpieces like the Mona Lisa and the Winged Victory of Samothrace. Troy couldn't help but watch her as she admired the artwork, her genuine awe and curiosity making him fall even more in love with her.

After the tour, they took a leisurely stroll along the Seine River, fingers intertwined as they soaked in the romance of Paris. The gentle ripples of the water reflected the golden hues of the afternoon sun, creating a picturesque moment of serenity. From there, they made their way to Montmartre, where the vibrant energy of the district was impossible to resist. The streets buzzed with life; artists skillfully capturing portraits in the square, musicians filling the air with enchanting melodies, and the irresistible aroma of freshly baked crêpes drifting from nearby cafés. The atmosphere was electric, yet undeniably charming, wrapping them in the magic of the city.

They stopped at a café with outdoor seating, ordering coffee and a Nutella-filled crepe to share. As they sipped their drinks, they watched the world go by, feeling like they were in the middle of a romantic movie.

"This place is magical," Love said, resting her chin in her hand as she looked around.

Troy nodded. "It is, but it's only magical because you're here with me."

Love smiled; her heart full. "I can't imagine being anywhere else but by your side."

As the sun began to dip in the sky, casting a golden glow over the city, they headed back to their hotel, hand in hand. Their hearts were full, and their love felt even stronger after a day of shared adventures.

When they returned to their suite, the concierge had left a small note congratulating them again on their honeymoon, along with a chilled bottle of FRE Moscato and a tray of macarons. Love grinned, holding up the note for Troy to see.

"I think Paris is trying to spoil us," she said with a laugh.

"Well, it's working," Troy replied, popping the champagne. "To us, Love. To our adventures, and to a lifetime of moments like these."

"To us," Love echoed, clinking her glass against his.

Wrapped in a blanket together, watching the Eiffel Tower sparkle against the night sky. Their hearts were filled with gratitude for the day and anticipation for the days yet to come.

Troy pulled her closer into his arms, swaying gently to the soft music playing on the streets of the city. Love melted into his embrace, her head resting against his chest as she listened to the steady rhythm of his heartbeat.

"You make everything feel so perfect," she whispered, looking up at him.

He brushed a strand of hair from her face, his fingertips trailing lightly down her cheek. "That's because I have you."

Troy lifted her effortlessly, carrying her to the bed, where they continued to lose themselves in each other, their love unfolding in the most intimate and beautiful way. Every touch, every whispered word, was a promise—of forever, of faithfulness, and of a love that would only continue to grow.

Wrapped in each other's arms, they eventually drifted into a peaceful sleep, the sound of the ocean outside their window a gentle lullaby to end a perfect day.

CHAPTER 5

Day 4

Their last day in Paris arrived far too quickly. The golden morning light spilled through the sheer curtains of their hotel room, casting a warm glow over the crisp white sheets. Love woke up to find Troy already awake, watching her with a warm smile. The city had woven its magic around them, filling their days with wonder and their nights with whispered dreams beneath the stars.

"Morning, beautiful," he murmured, brushing a stray loc from her face.

She smiled sleepily. "Morning. I think Paris has officially stolen my heart."

Troy chuckled. "Mine too. But I have a feeling today is going to make us fall even more in love with it."

Love propped herself up on her elbow. "And what exactly do you have planned, Mr. Hayes?"

He grinned, pulling her closer. "You'll see. But first, breakfast in bed."

As if on cue, a soft knock came at the door, and moments later, the scent of fresh strawberries, blueberries, eggs, polenta, sliced breakfast steak, croissants, rich coffee, and sweet jam filled the air. Love let out a delighted sigh and a warm smile.

"Okay," she said, sitting up as Troy handed her a cup of coffee. "Paris, you win."

He lifted his own cup in agreement. "To our last unforgettable day. I'm just making sure Paris keeps working its magic on you."

She clinked her cup against his, already eager to see what new memories the city had in store for them.

She took a bite, letting out a delighted sigh. "Mission accomplished."

They ate leisurely, savoring not just the food but the quiet intimacy of the morning. Sunlight spilled through the open balcony doors, carrying the distant hum of the city waking up. They finished breakfast and got dressed, dressing in matching color of Khaki colored tops and Jeans.

With Love standing beside him, hand in hand, Troy took one more sip of his coffee, then leaned in with a teasing glint in his eyes. "Now, are you ready for your surprise?"

Love raised an eyebrow. "That depends—am I going to love it?"

He brushed a kiss against her lips. "Without a doubt."

Intrigued, she set her cup down. "Then lead the way, Husband."

With a grin, Troy took her hand, and together, they stepped out from their suite. The elevator ride was quick then out the front door of the hotel they headed into the heart of Paris, ready for one last unforgettable adventure.

Hand in hand, Love and Troy strolled along the Seine, through the charming Parisian streets, their hands intertwined as the city buzzed around them and the distant melody of a street musician's violin drifted through the air, wrapping around them like a love song the golden hues of the late afternoon sun painting the water in warm reflections the morning air carried the scent of fresh pastries and blooming flowers, but Love was too focused on the anticipation building in her chest.

"Are you going to tell me where we're going yet?" she asked, narrowing her eyes at Troy.

He chuckled, shaking his head. "Patience, my Love. Just trust me."

Minutes later, they arrived at a secluded dock along the Seine, where a sleek private boat awaited them. A gentleman in a crisp white uniform stood nearby, ready to assist. Love gasped in surprise.

"Troy…" she breathed, turning to him.

He grinned. "Surprise."

Troy stepped in the boat, turned and extended his hand. Love grabbed Troy's hand and stepped onto the boat, where a cozy seating area was set up just for them. A small table held a chilled bottle of non-alcoholic Chardonnay and a tray of delicate French pastries. They sat and cuddled together under a soft blanket as the boat glided smoothly along the river, giving them a breathtaking view of the historic bridges and elegant architecture lining the Seine.

Love nestled next to Troy; her heart full. "This is perfect," she whispered as they drifted beneath the iconic Pont Alexandre III.

Troy pressed a kiss to her temple. "It gets better."

After a peaceful ride, the boat docked near a hidden entrance to a secluded garden. Love gasped as they stepped onto a cobblestone path leading to a breathtaking secret oasis with lush greenery, cascading flowers, and a quiet fountain tucked between the trees.

At the center of it all was a beautifully arranged picnic, complete with a soft blanket, pillows, chilled Fre Moscato wine and an assortment of French delicacies like cheeses, fruit, baguettes, delicate macarons, eclairs and soft buttery cake.

Love turned to Troy, eyes shimmering. "You really planned all this?"

He cupped her face gently. "For you? Anytime and always."

She let out a soft laugh, overwhelmed with gratitude and love. "I don't even have words."

"Then don't say anything," he whispered. "Just enjoy" he leaned down and kissed her softly on her lips."

They sank onto the blanket together, the soft rustling of leaves and distant hum of Parisian life surrounding them. Troy poured some Fre Moscato and passed a glass to Love. As they clinked their glasses together, Love knew this moment would forever be etched in her heart—an amazing honeymoon written in the heart of Paris.

"I don't want to leave," Love admitted, squeezing Troy's hand. "It feels like Paris became a part of us."

Troy nodded, pulling her closer. "I know what you mean. But maybe that's the beauty of it all, this city will always be ours in a way. Every time we think of Paris, we'll remember the amazing start to our beautiful honeymoon."

She smiled, resting her head against his shoulder. "Then we'll just have to come back."

"Absolutely," Troy agreed. "Maybe for an anniversary. Or maybe just because we can't stay away." "I look forward to more trips here with you baby," Love said, looking Troy in the eyes."

After their wonderful picnic they took their private boat back to the other side of the Seine.

As they headed back to the hotel, they made their way to one last stop, the Eiffel Tower. Standing beneath its dazzling lights, Love let out a soft sigh, taking in the breathtaking sight one last time.

Troy turned to her, his expression tender. "Before we go, there's one more thing."

She looked up at him, curiosity dancing in her eyes. "What's that?"

He reached into his pocket and pulled out a small lock, engraved with their initials. "I know they took down the original love locks from the bridge, but I found a spot where people still leave them."

Love took in a breath as she took the lock from his hand, tracing their initials with her fingers.

"Let's leave a piece of us here," he said softly. "A reminder that no matter where life takes us, Paris will always be a part of our love story."

With a shared smile, they fastened the lock onto the railing near the tower, sealing a promise between them and their time in Paris.

As they walked away, their fingers intertwined, Love glanced back one last time. Paris had given them memories they would cherish forever and ever but they are on to more adventure.

After a final morning in Paris, Love and Troy returned to their hotel to pack their bags, preparing for the next leg of their journey. As they stepped into the lobby, they exchanged heartfelt goodbyes with the wonderful staff who had made their stay so memorable.

Before leaving, they stopped by the hotel's front desk to hand over the suite keys. At that moment Vincent greeted them with a warm smile and handed them a neatly wrapped to-go box filled with delicate pastries—cannoli, éclairs, and macarons. "A little something sweet for your journey," he said.

"Thank you, Vincent," Love said, touched by the gesture. "And for all the amazing meals during our stay." Troy nodded in agreement.

"It was truly our pleasure," Vincent replied with a gracious nod.

Meanwhile, Charles had already taken their bags to the car waiting outside, and Sam stood by the back door, ready to assist. As they approached, Sam gave them a courteous nod and opened the door.

Love slid into the plush seat, and Troy followed, pausing briefly to nod at Sam. "Appreciate you, man," he said sincerely before Sam shut the door behind them.

As the car pulled away, Love looked out at the Parisian streets one last time, her heart full. Troy reached for her hand, giving it a gentle squeeze.

The drive to Charles de Gaulle Airport felt like the closing of the first part of the beautiful chapter called the Hayes Honeymoon. Paris had given them moments they would treasure forever, but on to a new adventure, one filled with golden sands, towering skyscrapers, and endless possibilities.

Dubai, here we come.

CHAPTER 6

Dubai Day 1

Love and Troy boarded their flight to Dubai. "I can't believe we're actually going to Dubai," Love said excitedly as they settled into their first-class seats.

Troy smiled, watching the excitement dance in her eyes. "I told you this honeymoon is all about unforgettable moments."

As the plane took off, Love gazed out the window, realizing she may have conquered her fear of flying, watching the Parisian skyline disappear beneath the clouds. Troy gently laced his fingers with hers. "Paris was just the beginning," he murmured.

She turned to him, smiling. "So, what's on the itinerary for Dubai, Mr. Romantic?"

He smirked. "You'll see."

After hours in the air, they finally descended into the dazzling city of Dubai. From above, the skyline shimmered like a sea of stars, the towering skyscrapers illuminated against the desert night.

The moment they stepped off the plane, a wave of warm air embraced them, carrying the subtle scent of oud and adventure. As they made their way through the airport to the exit doors, they spotted a chauffeur holding a sleek sign with their names printed in elegant script.

Approaching him, Troy offered a friendly smile. "Hello, your name please?"

"My name is Omar," the driver replied with a polite nod.

"Nice to meet you, Omar," Troy and Love said in unison.

With professional ease, Omar opened the door to the hotel's private limousine, and they slid into the luxurious interior, settling in for the ride.

As the car glided through the city streets, Love gazed out in awe. The futuristic skyline stretched endlessly before them, each building glowing like a masterpiece of modern art. The Burj Khalifa, the world's tallest skyscraper, stood tall among them, piercing the sky like a beacon of dreams.

Troy glanced at Love, watching the wonder in her eyes.

She turned to him, a smile playing on her lips. "I have a feeling this is going to add to an unforgettable moment."

As the limo continued toward their hotel, the city pulsed with life around them, promising great adventures ready to be experienced. "Before we start making memories in Dubai, I have something for you," Troy said with a warm smile, handing Love a small box.

Curious, she opened it to find three beautifully crafted charms for her Pandora bracelet: the Eiffel Tower, a Bible, and a picnic basket. Her eyes widened in surprise, and she let out a delighted gasp.

"Troy, you are full of surprises!" she exclaimed, her voice brimming with excitement.

He reached for her hand, gently unclasping her bracelet. "Each of these represents a special moment we've shared," he said as he carefully added the charms. Once they were secure, he fastened the bracelet back onto her wrist.

Love gazed down at it, her heart swelling with emotion. Each charm told a story—a treasured memory of their honeymoon. She grinned up at Troy, her eyes shining with love.

"I love it," she whispered, running her fingers over the new additions.

"And I love you," Troy replied, pulling her into a tender embrace as they prepared for yet another unforgettable adventure.

Their car pulled up to the luxurious Burj Al Arab, its iconic sail-shaped silhouette glowing brilliantly under the moonlight. The golden lights reflected off the calm waters below, making the entire scene look like something out of a dream.

Love held her breath as she took it all in. "Troy…" she whispered, awe-struck.

He grinned, watching her reaction with satisfaction. "Welcome to Dubai babe."

As they stepped out of the limo, the warm evening breeze carried the hum of the city's vibrant nightlife. The skyline sparkled in the distance, and the rhythmic waves of the Arabian Gulf lapped against the shore, adding to the magic of the moment.

Troy grabbed Love's hand and headed inside; they walked through the grand entrance of the hotel. The opulent lobby greeted them with towering gold pillars, intricate mosaic designs, and the delicate scent of fresh roses lingering in the air. Love inhaled deeply, her heart swelling with excitement.

She turned to Troy, eyes filled with anticipation. "I know you have something incredible planned," she said, a playful smile tugging at her lips.

Troy chuckled, wrapping an arm around her waist. "You'll just have to wait and see, Love. Let the fun begin, he said."

After a smooth check-in, a private butler, Jon, escorted Love and Troy to their suite, one of the most luxurious in the Burj Al Arab. As the double doors swung open, Love gasped.

The suite was breathtaking. A grand spiral staircase led to the second level, while floor-to-ceiling windows offered a panoramic view of the Arabian Gulf, where the moonlight danced over the waves. Plush velvet furniture, golden accents, and fresh Calla Lilies added to the elegance, making the space feel like a dream.

Troy stepped behind her, wrapping his arms around her waist. "Do you like it?" he whispered.

Love turned in his embrace, looking up at him with wide eyes. "Like it? Troy, this is beyond anything I could have imagined, and I see my favorite flowers adding to the room a beautiful ambiance."

He kissed her cheek and told her to get ready to enjoy every moment in Dubai.

Just then, a soft knock at the door announced the arrival of their private dining experience. Given the late hour, just shy of 11 p.m., they had opted for a light yet elegant meal.

A waiter wheeled in a beautifully arranged tray featuring grilled salmon and shrimp, delicately placed atop a fresh bed of crisp salad. They also opted for vibrant tropical fruits. The aroma of citrus and herbs filled the air, adding to the serene ambiance of the night.

Troy pulled out a chair for Love on their private terrace, where the city's skyline shimmered against the darkened sky. The warm breeze carried the distant hum of waves, making the moment feel even more surreal.

"A perfect late-night feast," Love said, picking up her fork with a contented sigh.

Troy nodded, pouring them each a glass of sparkling grape juice. "Light, fresh, and just enough to keep us dreaming of all the adventures ahead."

They clinked glasses, savoring both the meal and the magic of the night.

As they ate, they spoke in soft, unhurried tones about Paris, about the beauty of Dubai, and about the excitement of everything still to come. And as Love leaned back in her chair, completely relaxed and lost in that moment, she knew it was about to be a great four days.

Troy leaned in kissing her passionately, looking at her in her eyes saying, "And it's only the first night." They finally made their way inside, ready to enjoy the night and each other. After refreshing themselves from their travels, Love curled up beside Troy in the plush king-sized bed, the city lights of Dubai casting a soft glow through the windows. The warmth of his embrace surrounded her, and as the night deepened, so did the romance between them.

Troy brushed a gentle kiss against her forehead, his fingertips tracing slow, reverent patterns along her arm. "I still can't believe we're here," he murmured, his voice rich with love and gratitude.

Love gazed up at him, her heart full. "Me neither," she whispered. "But I wouldn't want to be anywhere else."

CHAPTER 7

Day 2

As the golden morning sun peeked through the floor-to-ceiling windows, Love lay beneath the soft sheets, feeling the warmth of a new day embracing her. She began to pray for her and Troy and their day's events asking God to guide wherever they may go and God to lead them.

She turned to find Troy already awake, leaning against the headboard, watching her with a soft smile.

"Good morning, beautiful," he murmured, brushing a strand of hair from her face.

She smiled sleepily. "Good Morning... I could wake up to this view forever." The view from their suite was breathtaking crystal-clear waters stretched endlessly, reflecting the sky in shades of blue and gold.

"You mean the Dubai skyline and waters or me?" Troy teased, arching an eyebrow.

Love giggled, stretching. "All three, but more of my handsome husband."

As Troy leaned in for a kiss just then, a gentle knock at the door signaled the arrival of their breakfast. The butler, Jon, entered, rolling in a lavish spread—fluffy croissants, golden waffles drizzled with honey, more fresh tropical fruits, and a steaming pot of Arabic coffee.

Troy thanked Jon and tiped him for his kindness.

Love's eyes widened. "This is incredible, love it."

"A little fuel for the day ahead," he said, pouring each of them a cup of coffee. "Because we have a full itinerary, Love."

She raised an eyebrow. "Oh? And what's first?"

He smirked. "Ever been in a Rolls-Royce before?"

Her lips parted in surprise. "No sir..."

Troy grinned. "Our ride for the day is waiting downstairs."

Excitement bubbled in Love's chest as she hurriedly ate and got ready. Today was going to be exciting.

After a delightful breakfast, Love and Troy stepped out of the Burj Al Arab, where a sleek black Rolls-Royce Phantom awaited them. Their driver, Omar, dressed in a crisp suit, opened the door with a polite nod.

Love slid into the plush leather seat, running her fingers over the soft interior. "Troy, this is unreal."

Troy smirked. "Only the best for you, Love. Now, let's go spoil you a little."

The drive to Dubai Mall, the world's largest shopping and entertainment destination, was mesmerizing. Love gazed out at the breathtaking sky, marveling at the sheer grandeur of the city. Within minutes, they arrived, greeted by towering glass structures and the shimmering waters of the Dubai Fountain.

Stepping inside, Love was immediately overwhelmed by the sheer opulence, the grand chandeliers, marble floors, and endless rows of high-end designer boutiques.

Troy took her hand. "Where to first? Chanel? Louis Vuitton? Dior?"

Love laughed. "I think I might faint before I even decide."

Their first stop was Chanel, where Love tried on a stunning white quilted handbag with gold accents.

"This is gorgeous," she breathed, admiring herself in the mirror.

Troy walked up behind her, already handing the sales associate his card. "It's yours."

Love turned to him, wide-eyed. "Troy! You don't have to..."

He leaned in, whispering, "I want to."

From there, they wandered through Gucci, Coach, and Hermès, where Troy insisted on buying Love a delicate diamond bracelet that sparkled under the boutique lights.

After a few more stops, they took a break at a private VIP lounge, where chilled refreshments and gourmet chocolates awaited them.

Love sighed, sinking into a velvet chair. "I have never been this spoiled in my life."

Troy chuckled, placing a kiss on her hand. "Get used to it, Love. You deserve it all."

As they sipped their drinks, Love smiled saying to herself this is one for the books.

After their short break in the VIP lounge, Love and Troy continued their shopping spree, stepping into Louis Vuitton next. Love's eyes lit up as she ran her fingers over the iconic handbags, admiring the craftsmanship.

"What do you think of this one?" she asked, holding up a sleek black leather tote with gold hardware.

Troy tilted his head, studying it. "It's beautiful, but..." He walked over to another display, picking up a limited-edition blush pink bag with a delicate gold chain. "This one feels more like you."

Love's heart melted. "You really pay attention to my style."

Troy smirked. "Of course. I know my woman."

Before Love could protest, he signaled the associate. "We'll take them both."

Next, they strolled into Dior, where Love fell in love with an elegant pair of nude stilettos.

"Troy, these are dreamy," she gushed, slipping one on.

Troy grinned. "Then they're coming home with us."

Love playfully nudged him. "You have to let me buy something on my own!"

Troy shook his head. "Not happening today. This is my treat to you."

From there, they moved to Cartier, where Love tried on a delicate rose gold Love bracelet. Troy watched her with admiration as she turned her wrist, the diamonds catching the light.

"This one," he said firmly. "You need something that reminds you of today, of us."

Love blushed as the associate fastened the bracelet around her wrist. "This is the most thoughtful gift ever."

Troy smiled, "Anything for you, my love!"

Before they left, Troy decided to treat himself too, purchasing a sleek Bulova watch that gleamed against his wrist.

Finally, they ended their shopping spree at Van Cleef & Arpels, where Love spotted a delicate butterfly pendant necklace.

"I love this," she whispered, touching the charm.

Troy didn't hesitate. "Wrap it up."

As they exited the store, their hands full of designer bags, Love leaned into Troy with a contented sigh. "I think I've had my fill of shopping for a lifetime."

Troy chuckled. "Oh, we're just getting started."

Love laughed. "You're impossible."

He kissed her lips. "Only for you, Love."

With their luxury finds in tow, they headed back toward their Rolls-Royce, ready for the next part of their unforgettable day in Dubai.

After their extravagant shopping spree, Love and Troy were whisked away in their Rolls-Royce to their next destination: a romantic lunch at Pierchic, one of Dubai's most exclusive overwater restaurants.

As they arrived, Love was thrilled and in awe. The restaurant, set on a private pier extending over the Arabian Gulf, offered a stunning panoramic view of the Burj Al Arab and the endless blue waters.

"Troy, this is stunning," she whispered as they were led to their private table at the edge of the deck, where the gentle sea breeze danced around them.

Troy pulled out her chair before settling across from her. "I wanted something special for us."

A waiter arrived with a bottle of chilled sparkling juice, pouring them each a glass.

"To love, to adventure, and to moments like these," Troy said, raising his glass.

"To us," Love echoed, clinking her glass against his.

They dined on a lavish spread of fresh lobster risotto, seared scallops, and truffle-infused prawns, each bite bursting with flavor. Love savored the moment and the way Troy looked at her as if she was the most beautiful thing in the world.

For dessert, they shared a decadent gold-leaf chocolate fondant, and petit fours that melted in their mouths with every bite.

"This is the best meal I've ever had," Love said, resting her hand over Troy's.

"Just wait until we get to our next stop," he said with a playful smirk.

After lunch, their driver took them to Downtown Dubai, where the Burj Khalifa, the tallest building in the world, towered above them.

Love craned her neck, staring up at the incredible structure. "I can't believe we're actually going up there."

Troy chuckled. "And not just to any floor—we're going all the way to the VIP Lounge on the 148th floor."

Love's mouth dropped. "The 148th floor? Babe, whew, I'm nervous to be that high up." She exhaled, already feeling the anticipation build in her chest.

Troy pulled her close, his arms wrapping securely around her. "I got you, babe," he whispered, the protector in him surfacing naturally. "You're safe with me."

She looked up into his reassuring gaze and nodded, finding comfort in his presence. As they stepped into the sleek elevator, the doors closed with a soft chime, and the ascend began.

The elevator doors slid open with a soft ding, revealing the breathtaking VIP Lounge on the 148th floor. The space was pure elegance, glass walls stretched from floor to ceiling, offering an unparalleled panoramic view of Dubai. Plush seating, dim ambient lighting, and soft Arabic music in the background made the atmosphere feel intimate and exclusive.

Love took a step forward, her eyes widening as she gazed at the city lights twinkling below like a sea of stars.

"Troy, this is unreal," she breathed, pressing a hand to the glass.

Troy stepped behind her, his arms sliding around her waist. "I knew you'd love it."

A friendly host approached them, offering signature dates and Arabic coffee—a traditional Emirati welcome. Love took a small sip, savoring the rich, spiced flavors.

"Delicious," she murmured, looking over at Troy, who was admiring her more than the view.

As the sun began its slow descent, the city bathed in hues of gold, orange, and purple. From their vantage point, they could see The Dubai Fountain, its jets dancing in synchronized harmony, the Burj Al Arab in the distance, and even the endless dunes of the desert stretching toward the horizon.

"I feel like we're floating above the world," Love whispered.

Troy gently turned her to face him, brushing a loc from her face. "You are, Love."

She smiled, her heart swelling with emotion. "You always know how to make me feel so special."

He kissed her forehead softly. "Because you are."

They lingered in the lounge, soaking in the once-in-a-lifetime view, holding each other close as the city sparkled beneath them.

After a while, Troy leaned in and asked. "Ready to head back to the hotel?"

Love grinned, yes baby." She looked at him, "you always make me feel so special babe!"

Troy smirked. "Always."

After their breathtaking experience at the Burj Khalifa, Troy and Love made their way back to their hotel, the Burj Al Arab, still wrapped in the magic of the night. As their luxury car pulled up to the grand entrance, Love let out a contented sigh, her fingers still laced with Troy's.

"That was incredible," she murmured, leaning into his side.

Troy kissed Love. "And the best part? The night's not over yet."

They stepped into the lobby, where the soft aroma of fresh roses filled the air. As they reached their suite, Love gasped, the room had been prepared for a night of pure romance.

Love turned to Troy, her eyes shining. "You planned all this?"

Troy smirked, taking her hand. "Every bit of it."

She wrapped her arms around his neck. "You never stop making me feel special."

He leaned in, his lips brushing against hers. "That's because you are, and I never will."

Love's eyes widened with delight as she took in the massage tables set up near the balcony, where two professional masseurs stood, waiting to give them the ultimate relaxation experience.

She turned to Troy, a playful smirk on her lips. "You really thought of everything, huh?"

Troy grinned, slipping off his jacket. "I wanted tonight to be perfect for you." He stepped closer, brushing a stray curl from her face. "You deserve to be pampered, Love."

A warm shiver ran down her spine, not just from the anticipation of the massage, but from the way he always made her feel so cherished.

They changed into their silk robes preparing for their couple massages.

The masseurs gestured for them to lay down, and as Love and Troy settled onto their respective massage tables, the soft aroma of lavender and jasmine oils filled the air. The gentle pressure of expert hands began working out every ounce of tension in their bodies, melting away any remaining stress from their travels.

Love let out a satisfied sigh. "This is heaven."

Troy chuckled, his voice slightly muffled as he rested his head on the plush headrest. "Told you."

The combination of warm oils, skilled hands, and the soothing background music created an atmosphere of pure bliss. The balcony doors were slightly open, letting in a soft ocean breeze as they indulged in the peaceful moment together.

After nearly an hour of deep relaxation, the massages ended. They put their robes back on. The masseurs quietly left, leaving them feeling completely rejuvenated.

Troy reached for Love's hand. "Feeling good?"

She turned her head to look at him, her expression dreamy. "Better than good. I feel like I'm floating."

He smiled, sitting up and pulling her into his arms. "Then let's float together."

Still wrapped in a serene haze, they decided to move toward the private Jacuzzi on their balcony, where warm bubbling water awaited them. Slipping into the soothing embrace of the Jacuzzi, Love rested against Troy's chest, gazing out at the Dubai sky twinkling in the night.

"This is the best way to end the night," she murmured.

Troy kissed her temple. "And tomorrow, we will wake up to more surprises."

Love smiled, knowing that with him, every day was a dream come true. After about an hour they got out of the jacuzzi wrapped in towels.

"I feel like I'm living in a dream," she whispered.

Troy wrapped his arms around her from behind. "Then let's never wake up."

They stood in comfortable silence, savoring the moment, the cool night breeze wrapping around them. Eventually, they moved inside, where they indulged in the decadent strawberries and shared quiet laughter over memories of the day.

As the night deepened, they showered together then curled up together in the plush bed, wrapped in warmth, love, and the certainty that their journey together was only getting better.

"Goodnight, my love," Troy whispered, pressing a soft kiss to her lips.

Love smiled, her eyes fluttering closed. "Goodnight, babe."

And with that, they drifted off to sleep, hearts full and dreams endless.

CHAPTER 8

Day 3

As the first rays of the sun peeked over the horizon, casting a golden glow over Dubai, Troy and Love awoke to the soft sounds of ocean waves and distant birds.

Love stretched, smiling as she turned toward Troy. "Good morning, handsome."

Troy smirked, pulling her closer. "Good morning, beautiful. Ready for another unforgettable day?"

She nodded, and just then, a knock at the door signaled the arrival of their romantic sunrise breakfast.

Troy led Love up to their private rooftop terrace, where an elegant breakfast awaited them. A white linen table was adorned with fresh flowers, candles, and silverware, all overlooking the stunning Arabian Gulf as the sun rose, painting the sky in hues of pink, orange, and gold.

The private chef, Ali, greeted them warmly. "Good morning, Mr. Troy, Mrs. Love. Today's menu includes fluffy croissants and brioche, crepes, lobster benedict, fresh fruit platters, honey-drizzled yogurt, smoked salmon, and a selection of tropical juices."

Love's eyes sparkled. "This is absolutely breathtaking."

They sipped on freshly squeezed mango and passion fruit juice, enjoying each bite of their luxurious meal while soaking in the view.

As the sun fully emerged, Troy reached across the table, taking Love's hand. "Baby you are breathtaking and every sunrise with you feels like a new beginning."

She smiled softly. "And I wouldn't want to start my day with anyone else."

After breakfast, they changed into comfortable beach attire and headed down to the private shoreline of their hotel. The powdery white sand was cool beneath their feet as they walked hand in hand, waves gently lapping at their toes.

Love giggled as Troy playfully splashed water at her. "Oh, you're asking for it now!" She scooped up a handful of water and threw it back at him.

Troy laughed, wrapping his arms around her waist and spinning her around. "Truce, truce!"

They slowed their pace, enjoying the peaceful morning breeze, the sound of the ocean, and the warmth of being wrapped in each other's presence.

As they walked further along the shore, Love noticed something unusual in the distance—a hot air balloon, its vibrant colors standing out against the clear blue sky.

She turned to Troy, eyes wide. "No way... are we doing this?"

Troy grinned. "What better way to see Dubai than from the sky?"

After a short scenic walk, they arrived at a secluded launch site, where a massive hot air balloon stood waiting, its basket lined with plush seating for their private experience.

Love's heart pounded with excitement as they stepped inside. The pilot greeted them, and soon, the balloon lifted off the ground, gently ascending above the endless golden dunes.

Love gasped as she took in the breathtaking view, the desert stretched out as far as the eye could see, the beautiful, bright sun casting dramatic shadows over the sand.

Troy wrapped an arm around her waist. "You're not nervous, are you?"

She shook her head. "Not with you here."

Up in the sky, with the world quiet and still, they shared a tender kiss, the moment feeling like something out of a dream.

After an hour ride as they made a full 360 of the beach and desert they descended and landed back at the landing pad. By the time they came back it was right at 1130a.m. They slowly walked back to their hotel suite. They got back around Noon and decided to shower and change. As soon as they got dressed there was a knock on the door.

A waiter wheeled in a lavish lunch spread grilled lobster, saffron-infused rice, juicy lamb kebabs, and an assortment of fresh fruits and desserts. The scent of exotic spices filled the air, making Love's mouth water.

They moved to the elegantly set table on their private terrace. Love sighed as she took in the views of Dubai.

"Lunch in the warm Dubai weather is awesome! You really thought of everything," she said, picking up her glass of sparkling fruit juice.

Troy smirked. "Only the best for you."

They clinked glasses, the soft clatter blending with the distant sound of chatter of tourists and waves of the water. As they ate, they talked about their excitement for the amazing times they have had up to this point so much so they can't even put it into many words.

After lunch, Troy stood and held out his hand. "Dance with me?"

Love laughed softly. "There's no music."

He pulled her close, swaying gently. "We don't need it."

They danced slowly and effortlessly, as if time itself had paused just for them. With each graceful step, their bodies moved in perfect harmony, swaying to a rhythm that seemed to exist only between them. The world around them faded into a blur; there was no rush, no noise, no distractions, just the warmth of their embrace and the steady beat of their hearts. Eyes locked, smiles soft, they surrendered to the moment, allowing love to lead them across the floor like a gentle whisper.

After they freshen up, Troy had their final evening set for their final romantic experience of the day—a private yacht dinner under the stars.

Dressed in elegant evening attire as they stepped outside, a sleek black Rolls-Royce was already waiting for them. The driver opened the door, and as Love slid in, she turned to Troy with a playful smile. "Okay, Mr. Romantic, where to now?"

Troy grinned, placing a hand on her thigh. "You'll see."

The ride was smooth, the sun casting a golden glow as it dipped lower in the sky as they drove toward the marina. Love watched as they approached Dubai Harbor, where a luxurious white private yacht awaited them.

Her mouth dropped. "Troy... no way."

He chuckled, stepping out of the car and holding his hand out to her. "Yes way. Come on, Love."

A crew member in an elegant white uniform welcomed them aboard the 75-foot luxury yacht, leading them to the upper deck, where a beautifully set candlelit table awaited them. A gentle breeze carried the scent of the ocean as the yacht slowly pulled away from the marina, gliding over the calm waters.

"This is straight out of a dream," Love whispered, looking around at the glowing city skyline. Troy pulled out her chair. "Then let's make it a night you'll never forget."

Additional crew members welcomed them warmly as they embarked on their five-star dining experience, beginning with Crab Rangoon hors d'oeuvres paired with a chilled bottle of Fre Moscato. Next came their appetizers—crispy, golden falafel—followed by fresh, crisp salads designed to cleanse their palates in preparation for the main course.

Between courses, they enjoyed a leisurely ten-minute break, savoring the flavors and sharing their thoughts on each dish. The pause also allowed the serving staff to clear the table, refresh their silverware, and ensure the next course was presented at its peak of freshness.

The private chef came out with the serving staff to present the exquisite meal. Love had butter-seared lobster tail, grilled lamb chops, and a fresh Mediterranean Salad. Troy also chose a butter-seared lobster tail, medium well filet mignon and truffle mashed potatoes. Their meal paired with Fre Chardonnay. The yacht crew carefully curated an atmosphere of privacy and intimacy, allowing them to fully immerse themselves in the magic of the moment. Yet, one crew member remained nearby at a discreet distance, attentive and ready to assist should they need anything, ensuring seamless service without intruding on their experience.

As they dined, the yacht sailed smoothly, the city skyline shimmering in the distance along with the stars in the night sky.

Love leaned into Troy, a soft sigh escaping her lips. "This has been the most magical day."

Troy kissed her temple. "Yes, every moment has been amazing with you, Love."

After dinner, they moved to the lounge area, where a cozy setup with plush cushions and soft blankets awaited them. Love leaned into Troy's embrace as the yacht sailed past iconic landmarks—the Atlantis, The Palm, the Burj Al Arab, and the dazzling Ain Dubai Ferris wheel.

As they settled into their seats, the soft, enchanting notes of a violin filled the air. Their attention turned to a violinist nearby, gracefully playing a beautiful melody that added to the evening's magic. Once again, Troy turned to Love, extending his hand with a warm smile. "May I have this dance?" he asked.

"You think we could just stay out here forever?" Love sighed, as they swayed to the soft tones of the beautiful harmonic tones.

Troy kissed her softly. "If that's what you want, I'll make it happen."

She smiled, placing a hand over his heart. "I already have everything I want right here."

As the yacht continued its peaceful journey across the water, they sat in silence, completely lost in the moment—wrapped in love, adventure, and the magic of Dubai.

With the sound of gentle waves, the warm breeze in their hair, and their hearts overflowing with love, the night ended in the most perfect way just wrapped in each other's arms, lost in the beauty of their love and the joyous adventure they were living together.

As the yacht gently docked, Troy and Love reluctantly stepped off, still caught in the enchantment of the evening. A private car awaited them, ready to take them back to their hotel. The drive was quiet yet filled with warmth, their fingers intertwined as they replayed the night's unforgettable moments.

Back at their hotel, they stepped into the serene comfort of their suite, the city's glow peeking through the curtains. Love kicked off her heels with a contented sigh, while Troy loosened his collar, watching her with a soft smile. They moved through their nighttime routine unhurriedly, exchanging knowing glances and sweet laughter.

Slipping beneath the cool sheets, they found their way back into each other's arms, the world outside fading into silence. With whispered words of gratitude and love, they drifted off to sleep, their hearts full and at peace.

CHAPTER 9

Day 4

As the golden morning light filtered through the grand windows of their suite, Love and Troy woke up feeling refreshed and eager for another day of adventure in Dubai. After their morning devotion and prayer, they got ready for the day, dressed in stylish yet comfortable outfits perfect for exploring the city.

They started their day with a luxurious breakfast at ZEST, a stunning open-air restaurant at One & Only The Palm. The tranquil ambiance, surrounded by lush greenery and overlooking the Arabian Gulf, made for the perfect start to the morning.

Love savored a plate of fresh fruit, warm croissants, and honey-drizzled yogurt, while Troy enjoyed a perfectly cooked omelet, grilled halloumi, and a rich cup of Arabic coffee. They shared a plate of Shakshuka, a delicious dish of poached eggs in a spiced tomato sauce, enjoying every bite as the morning breeze carried the scent of fresh flowers.

Wanting to experience both the modern and historic sites of Dubai, they took a ride to Al Fahidi Historical District, walking through the narrow alleyways lined with traditional sand-colored buildings. They visited the Dubai Museum, learning about the city's transformation from a small fishing village to a global metropolis.

From there, they hopped on a wooden abra boat, gliding across Dubai Creek to explore the famous Gold and Spice Souks. The air was filled with the rich scents of saffron, cinnamon, and oud perfume.

Love was drawn to the stunning gold jewelry, admiring the craftsmanship, while Troy playfully bargained for a bottle of exquisite Arabian perfume for her.

In the afternoon, they went back to the hotel to change into light desert-friendly outfits and then out to embark on an exhilarating desert safari. The moment their luxury 4x4 vehicle hit the dunes, Love squealed in excitement as they sped up and down the golden waves of sand. Troy squeezed her hand, grinning at her reaction.

After dune bashing, they rode camelback through the dunes, taking in the stunning desert sunset. The sky transformed into a masterpiece of pink, orange, and deep purple hues. Love leaned against Troy, overwhelmed by the beauty of the moment.

As the sun dipped below the horizon, painting the desert sky in shades of amber and violet, they arrived at a breathtaking Bedouin-style camp nestled among the golden dunes. The moment felt like something out of a dream. Awaiting them was a private, romantic dinner set beneath a canopy draped with delicate fabrics and strung with glowing lanterns that swayed gently in the warm evening breeze.

The air was filled with the soft strains of traditional Arabian music, blending seamlessly with the crackle of the open fire and the distant rustle of the desert wind. Every detail of the evening had been crafted to perfection—low cushioned seating, ornate rugs underfoot, and the intoxicating aroma of spiced meats wafting through the air.

Their dinner was a feast fit for royalty. They shared platters of juicy grilled kebabs, fragrant saffron rice studded with nuts and raisins, warm flatbreads straight from the oven, and an array of flavorful dips. For dessert, they savored flaky, honey-drenched baklava and sipped mint tea as the stars began to blanket the sky.

Entertainment added a touch of magic to the night. Graceful belly dancers moved in rhythm with the music, their glittering costumes catching the light, while vibrant Tanoura dancers spun in endless circles, their skirts a blur of color and tradition. Love leaned into Troy, her head resting on his shoulder, completely enchanted.

In that sacred desert silence, wrapped in warmth, flavor, and rhythm, they shared glances that said everything—this was a memory they would never forget.

Returning to their luxurious hotel suite, Love and Troy stepped onto their private balcony, overlooking the dazzling Dubai skyline. The city lights reflected in their eyes as they clinked glasses of sparkling juice in celebration of another unforgettable day.

Troy pulled Love into his arms, swaying with her in a slow, intimate dance under the night sky. "Every day with you is a blessing," he whispered, brushing a soft kiss against her lips.

Love smiled, leaning into him. "And we have a lifetime of them to come."

Hand in hand, they retreated inside, the night unfolding into yet another cherished memory in their journey of love.

CHAPTER 10

MALDIVES
Day 1

Before the first light of dawn, the soft chime of an alarm stirred them awake. Though reluctant to leave the comfort of their embrace, they knew another journey awaited. With sleepy smiles and lingering touches, they prepared for the day ahead freshening up, packing their bags, and making sure they hadn't left anything behind.

By 5:30 a.m., they were en route to the airport, the city lights twinkling in the distance as they reflected on the unforgettable night. Hand in hand, they checked in, made their way through security, and found their gate. As the final boarding call echoed through the terminal, Troy pulled Love close, pressing a gentle kiss to her forehead.

"Ready for our next adventure?" he asked, his voice filled with excitement.

"With you?" Love smiled; her heart full. "Always."

At 7 a.m., they boarded their flight, settling into their seats as the plane prepared for 7:45 a.m. takeoff, another chapter of their honeymoon closing, and on to begin another. They took a moment to pray for a safe flight before taking off with feelings of joy and excitement in their stomachs as they head to their next location declaring their favorite travel scripture *(Deuteronomy 11:24)*.

Their 4-hour flight from Dubai was smooth, and the anticipation of their tropical destination only grew as the plane soared through the sky. They took time to spend time in devotion of God's word and discussing the story of Abraham and Sarah. How God still honored his word even in their old age. They smiled at that thought of God's faithfulness then and even in their lives.

As the plane glided through the air Love laid her head on Troy shoulder and closed her eyes. Troy knew this was the perfect moment. Love he whispered she lifted her head as he yet again handed her a box. Love's eyes widened in surprise as she took the small box from Troy's hands. She gently lifted the lid, her breath catching as she saw the three beautifully crafted charms nestled inside—a heart-shaped charm with one of their favorite picture from the wedding, a delicate Pandora shopping bag, and a whimsical hot air balloon.

"Troy…" she whispered, her voice laced with emotion as she traced her fingers over the charms.

"I wanted you to have something to always remember this trip and wedding by," he said, his eyes full of love. "Every charm tells a part of our journey, and there's still so much more to come."

Love smiled, holding out her wrist as Troy unclasped her bracelet, adding the new charms to the growing collection. Once he secured it back onto her wrist, she turned it over, admiring each meaningful piece.

"I love it," she said, pressing a soft kiss to his lips. "And I love you."

"I love you more," he whispered, brushing a thumb across her cheek.

With a content sigh, Love rested her head against his shoulder once more, feeling the warmth of his presence. As the plane continued soaring through the sky, she held onto his hand, her heart overflowing with gratitude and bliss.

When they landed in Male' they got their luggage and boarded a speed boat to get to their Maldive Resort, Love could hardly contain her excitement. Troy chose the all-inclusive package which included another private butler, endless dining options, a private patio, a view of the ocean on one side and garden on the other through the bay window. The island was a paradise—lush greenery, pristine white sand beaches, and the gentle sounds of the waves crashing against the shore.

As they arrived at their private villa over the water, Love looked around in awe at the breathtaking view. "Troy, this place is perfect. I can't believe you planned all of this." Each location felt different in its own exquisite way. This location just gave her the feeling of romance and relaxation.

Troy kissed her, his heart swelling with love as the reality of their marriage settled in. He cupped her face gently in his hands and, unable to resist, he kissed her passionately on the lips. "Only the best for you, Love. We deserve this and so much more. This is just the beginning of a start to this journey filled with this beautiful love."

Love stood still, her heart racing from the intensity of the kiss. A smile crept across her face as the thought echoed in her mind, *My husband*. It still felt surreal, but so incredibly right.

Troy pulled away slowly, his hands still lingering on her face, his eyes full of love and adoration. The world seemed to fade around them as they stood there, just the two of them, in that perfect moment.

Love's heart was racing, the warmth of the kiss still lingering on her lips. She placed her hand over his, feeling the steady beat of his heart beneath her palm. "I never thought I'd feel this way," she whispered, her voice soft and filled with awe. "Like everything I ever dreamed of is real now. You're my forever, Troy."

Troy smiled, his thumb brushing across her cheek. "And you're mine. I knew from the moment I met you that you were mine and God had a plan for us, and I'm so thankful every day that I get to walk through life with you by my side."

Love's eyes shone as she gazed up at him. "I feel so incredibly blessed to be your wife."

He leaned in again, his lips brushing against her lips as he whispered, "I'll spend the rest of my life making sure you know just how much you mean to me."

For a long moment, they stood there in the peace of their private paradise, simply being together. Everything about the world felt right in that instant, because Love and Troy knew that they had found something truly beautiful in each other. Their love, their faith, their future together was all just beginning and they were enjoying each and every moment..

As they held each other, the sound of the ocean waves blended with the rhythm of their hearts, both of them overwhelmed with gratitude for the love they had found.

They knew that the days on the island were going to be filled with adventure and relaxation. They planned to have walks along the beach, candlelit dinners under the stars, to explore the island's hidden waterfalls, each moment was a memory they shared.

They unpacked and settled into their villa. The first adventure was a guided tour at 2 p.m., learning about the island's rich history, culture, and breathtaking landscapes. They marveled at the lush greenery, the towering palm trees swaying in the breeze, and the crystal-clear waters stretching beyond the horizon.

Once they returned, they indulged in a delicious lunch at a charming beachfront café near their villa, savoring the fresh flavors of the island while listening to the soothing sound of the waves. Afterward, they spent the afternoon basking under the golden sun on their private open deck, letting the warmth embrace them before cooling off with a playful swim in the crystal-clear waters.

As part of their all-inclusive package, they received two complimentary jet skis. Troy, already experienced, took the time to teach Love how to ride. Once she got the hang of it, her competitive side emerged, and soon they were racing across the waves, laughter echoing over the water. At times, they simply drifted in the middle of the ocean, enjoying the stillness, deep conversations, and the beauty of being together.

As the sun began its descent, casting a golden glow over the sea, they reluctantly headed back to shore around 6 p.m., hearts full of yet another unforgettable day.

As the sun dipped toward the horizon, they strolled along the shoreline, the waves playfully lapping at their feet. The sky transformed into a breathtaking canvas of orange, pink, and purple—a divine masterpiece only God could paint. Fingers intertwined, they walked in peaceful harmony, soaking in the beauty around them. Laughter filled the air as families enjoyed the beach, children splashing in the ocean and chasing each other without a care in the world. It was a scene of pure joy, a reminder of life's simple blessings and the love that surrounded them.

As the last traces of sunlight faded into the horizon, they made their way back to their villa, the evening breeze cool against their sun-kissed skin. Once inside, they washed off the saltwater and changed into comfortable loungewear before stepping out onto their private deck.

They ate dinner on the deck under a sky full of twinkling stars and soft flights of their overhead string lights then they curled up together on a plush lounge chair, sipping on fresh coconut water and reminiscing about the beautiful memories they had created that day like how she earned how to jet ski and became a pro in one day. Soft music played in the background, blending seamlessly with the rhythmic sound of the waves.

Before heading to bed, they knelt together in prayer, thanking God for another day of love, laughter, and adventure. As they lay in bed, wrapped in each other's arms, Love whispered, "I never want this to end."

Troy kissed her gently. "With God leading us, we will make many great memories."

With hearts full of gratitude and love, they drifted into a peaceful sleep, ready to embrace whatever blessings the next day would bring.

CHAPTER 11

Day 2

As the sun peeked over the horizon, Love and Troy began their second day with their morning devotion, reading scripture and praying together as the soft sound of the waves set a peaceful tone for the day ahead. Afterward, they packed a backpack with snacks, water, and juice, grabbed some warm breakfast muffins and steaming coffee from the resort's café, and geared up for an exhilarating day of adventure.

Their first stop was zip-lining through the tropical rainforest. Standing atop the platform, Love felt a surge of nervous excitement. Troy gave her hand a reassuring squeeze. "We've got this, babe," he said, his eyes filled with encouragement.

Taking a deep breath, she took the leap, and in an instant, she was soaring through the air. The rush of wind against her face, the breathtaking canopy of lush green below—it was both thrilling and freeing. Troy followed close behind, laughing as he zipped across. Each time they leaped from one platform to the next, it reminded them of their trust in God—and in each other.

By midday, the thrill of their morning adventures had worked up a hearty appetite. The couple wandered through the lush greenery until they stumbled upon a hidden gem—a cozy jungle café nestled beneath the towering trees, its wooden deck extending over a tranquil lagoon. The soft rustling of leaves and the distant hum of tropical birds created a peaceful ambiance, making it feel like a secluded paradise.

As they approached, the scent of grilled seafood and fragrant spices filled the air, instantly making their stomachs growl. The friendly café owner, a warm-hearted woman with a kind smile, welcomed them and guided them to a table with a breathtaking view of the crystal-clear water. Tiny fish swam just beneath the surface, occasionally rippling the lagoon as they darted between the lily pads.

The menu featured an array of island delicacies, each dish crafted from fresh, locally sourced ingredients. After taking their orders, they sipped on freshly squeezed pineapple juice, letting the cool sweetness quench their thirst as they soaked in the serene surroundings.

Soon, their meal arrived—plump, perfectly grilled fish seasoned with aromatic herbs, served alongside a heaping portion of coconut rice that smelled of warm, nutty richness. A vibrant mango salad, bursting with color and flavor, added a refreshing contrast to the savory seafood.

Love took her first bite, her eyes widening in delight. "Oh my gosh, this is amazing," she murmured, savoring the explosion of flavors.

Troy nodded, his mouth full, giving her a thumbs-up in agreement. "Best meal yet," he said after swallowing.

They ate slowly, enjoying every bite, occasionally feeding each other small pieces and laughing when Love tried (and failed) to use her fork gracefully with the sticky coconut rice.

Halfway through their meal, the café owner stopped by with a plate of fried plantains drizzled with caramelized honey. "A little something extra, on the house," she said with a wink.

Love's face lit up. "Thank you so much!"

Troy chuckled, watching as Love eagerly took a bite of the crispy, golden plantains. "I think she just made your day," he teased.

She nodded happily. "Absolutely."

As they finished their meal, they leaned back in their chairs, completely satisfied. With full stomachs and content hearts, they lingered a little longer, taking in the beauty around them. It was more than just a lunch stop—it was a moment of pure peace, a chance to slow down and appreciate the simple joys of good food, breathtaking nature, and the love they shared.

After lunch, they sat and enjoyed the scenery for about an hour then they set off for their next adventure—ATV riding through rugged jungle trails. Love, always up for a challenge, quickly got the hang of maneuvering the vehicle, and soon, they were speeding through the winding paths, kicking up dirt as they laughed and raced each other. The thrill of the ride, mixed with the breathtaking scenery of dense foliage and hidden waterfalls, made it an unforgettable experience.

As the afternoon faded into evening, they slowed things down with a romantic horseback ride along the beach. The soft golden light of the setting sun reflected on the water as they trotted through the surf, the gentle waves rolling up to greet them. Love let out a contented sigh, her fingers running through her horse's mane.

Out of nowhere, she grinned and turned to Troy. "I've always wanted a horse. Can we get a farm now?"

Troy laughed, shaking his head. "Well, uh, where exactly are we going to keep the animals in the city, babe?"

"I don't know, I just want a horse now!" she said playfully, shrugging before giving her horse a gentle tap, urging it into a slow gallop.

Troy chuckled, tapping his own horse to catch up. "Okay, babe, if you're serious, we'll look into it."

Love giggled, knowing he was just humoring her. They continued their ride in comfortable silence, the rhythmic clopping of hooves and the soothing sound of the waves filling the air.

That night, they dined under the stars at the resort's elegant seaside restaurant. A candlelit table was set for two on the sand, the flickering flames casting a soft glow between them. The aroma of grilled lobster and buttery garlic shrimp filled the air as they clinked their glasses together.

"To adventure," Troy said with a smile.

"To us," Love added, her heart full.

As they enjoyed their meal, they reflected on the day's adventures—the thrills, the laughter, and the joy of experiencing it all together. It was more than just a day of adventure; it was another beautiful chapter in their love story.

After dinner, they went back to their villa hand in hand, the warmth of the island breeze wrapping around them like a comforting embrace. The rhythmic sound of the ocean waves accompanied their quiet conversation, their voices filled with love and gratitude.

Once inside their suite, the soft glow of candlelight flickered across the room, casting a golden hue over the elegant space. Love slipped off her sneakers, sighing as she stretched her tired feet, while Troy walked over to the garden tub and started their bathwater.

The soothing sound of water filling the tub echoed through the suite as Troy turned, catching Love's gaze. "Come here, baby," he murmured, holding out his hand. She stepped toward him, and he gently lifted her onto the vanity, removing her shoes completely and rubbing slow, tender circles into her sore feet.

She sighed, her eyes fluttering closed. "You always know exactly what I need."

Troy chuckled. "I pay attention." He kissed her ankle softly before standing to check the water temperature. He added a few drops of essential oils, and the calming aroma of lavender and vanilla filled the air.

Once the bath was ready, Troy helped Love out of her clothes, undressing himself as well before stepping into the warm, inviting water with her. He pulled her back against his chest, his arms wrapping securely around her waist as they both let out deep, contented sighs.

"This is perfect," Love whispered, tracing lazy circles on Troy's arm.

He kissed her shoulder. "You're perfect."

They sat in the tub, soaking off the tiredness of the adventures they had, allowing the warmth, the intimacy, and the quiet love to surround them. Love reached for his hand under the water, intertwining their fingers. "I still can't believe we're here, that this is our life."

Troy pressed a soft kiss to her temple. "Believe it, baby. Because this is just the beginning."

The water embraced them as they shared soft kisses, their connection deepening with every whispered word and lingering touch. When the water began to cool, Love stood. Troy got out the tub then lifted Love out, wrapping her in a plush robe before carrying her to bed.

The night unfolded in gentle, unhurried moments—kisses that spoke of devotion, touches that promised forever, and whispered words that sealed their love even deeper. As they lay wrapped in each other's arms, Love sighed in contentment.

"I love you, Troy."

He brushed his lips against her forehead. "I love you more."

With the sound of the waves crashing in the distance and their hearts beating in perfect harmony, they drifted into sleep, wrapped in love, warmth, and the promise of forever.

CHAPTER 12

Day 3

After two days of non-stop adventure, they dedicated their third day to relaxation. They began their day with a leisurely breakfast on the deck, overlooking the turquoise waters, the sun glistening off the surface. They ate fresh fruit, pastries, and sipped on freshly brewed coffee while sharing stories and laughter. After another peaceful morning of devotion, Love and Troy decided to take things at a slower pace. The day was filled with moments of tranquility, and they spent most of it relaxing by the beach and enjoying each other's company. The resort's luxury spa welcomed them with calming aromas and peaceful ambiance. They indulged in side-by-side massages, letting go of any tension and simply enjoying the serenity of the moment.

As the sun climbed higher into the sky, casting a golden glow over the resort, Troy and Love decided to spend the afternoon basking in the warmth of the tropical paradise. Hand in hand, they made their way to the infinity pool that overlooked the shimmering ocean, its crystal-clear water reflecting the endless blue of the sky.

They settled onto plush lounge chairs beneath the shade of swaying palm trees, the scent of salt and hibiscus lingering in the air. A server soon arrived, offering them cold, refreshing drinks—Troy opted for a chilled mango smoothie, while Love sipped on a coconut-infused iced tea. With each sip, the cool liquid was a perfect contrast to the warmth of the sun kissing their skin.

The gentle sound of the waves rolling onto the shore blended harmoniously with the faint music playing from the poolside speakers, creating a soothing backdrop for their lazy afternoon. They talked about everything and nothing—reminiscing on the beauty of their wedding, dreaming about their future together, and playfully teasing each other in the way only two people deeply in love could.

After a while, Love dipped her toes into the pool before slowly easing herself in, the cool water sending a refreshing chill up her spine. Troy followed, pulling her into his arms as they floated effortlessly, savoring the moment. As the sun reflected off the rippling water, their laughter echoed around them, pure and unfiltered, a melody of love and contentment.

With every passing hour, their connection deepened—not just in words, but in the quiet, simple joys of being together. The way Troy reached over to brush a stray curl from Love's face, the way her fingers lingered on his arm as she spoke, the shared smiles that needed no explanation. Time seemed to slow down as they embraced the beauty of the moment, savoring the peace, the love, and the undeniable blessing of having each other.

As the evening sun dipped lower on the horizon, painting the sky in brilliant shades of gold and crimson, Troy and Love stepped onto a sleek, private boat. The gentle rocking of the waves beneath them, combined with the salty breeze, created an air of tranquility as they set off toward a secluded part of the island. Hand in hand, they sat close, watching the sun's last rays dance across the water, their hearts full of gratitude for the beauty of the moment.

The short ride was peaceful, filled with quiet whispers and knowing smiles. As the boat approached the hidden cove, Love's eyes widened in delight. The shoreline was set up just for them—a beautifully adorned dining table sat in the sand, illuminated by a soft golden glow from twinkling fairy lights strung between two palm trees. Nearby, a cozy fire pit crackled gently, adding to the warmth of the setting. The waves lapped lazily against the shore, as if singing a lullaby to the night.

Troy helped Love off the boat, guiding her toward their intimate setup. A private chef, dressed in crisp white, greeted them with a warm smile before stepping aside to let them settle in. Love ran her fingers along the table setting—elegant yet simple, with fresh tropical flowers adding a vibrant touch.

As they took their seats, the scent of their meal filled the air. It was a feast of freshly caught fish, coconut rice infused with island spices, and an assortment of juicy tropical fruits. Love closed her eyes as she took her first bite, savoring the rich flavors that seemed to melt on her tongue. "This is incredible," she murmured, looking over at Troy, whose satisfied expression mirrored her own.

Between bites, they shared laughter, soft touches, and moments of quiet admiration for each other. As if the night couldn't get any more perfect, an acoustic guitarist appeared, his fingers dancing effortlessly over the strings, playing soft, melodic tunes that blended seamlessly with the rhythmic sounds of the ocean.

Troy reached for Love's hand, intertwining their fingers as they swayed slightly to the music. "Dance with me," he whispered, standing and gently pulling her into his embrace. Barefoot in the sand, under a sky full of stars, they moved together in perfect harmony, completely lost in each other.

As the night deepened, they lingered at their table, sipping on fresh coconut water and watching the waves glisten under the moonlight. It was more than just a dinner—it was a moment of pure, uninterrupted intimacy, a memory etched into their hearts forever.

The couple returned to their villa, their hearts full from the serenity of the day. They shared a long, warm shower together, the water cascading over them as they exchanged tender kisses, hands tracing familiar paths. The night was theirs to enjoy, and there was a peaceful calm that hung in the air.

Once in bed, with the soft glow of candles illuminating the room, they wrapped themselves in each other's arms. The gentle rhythm of their breathing synced as they whispered sweet words, taking time to truly be present with one another. There was no rush, just the simple joy of being together, of letting go of the world outside.

In the quiet of the night, Love's hand gently traced Troy's jawline. "I love you more than words can say," she whispered, her voice barely above a breath.

Troy smiled, pulling her closer. "I love you, too. More than you'll ever know."

Their kiss was slow and deep, a perfect reflection of the love they shared, sacred, unhurried, and full of promise. In that intimate moment, they let everything fade away, lost in the comfort of each other's presence. The day ended not with grand gestures, but with the kind of closeness that only deepens over time, leaving them both feeling completely at peace.

As they drifted into sleep, entwined in each other's arms.

CHAPTER 13

Day 4

The fourth day took them out to sea. They boarded a catamaran for a day of sailing across the turquoise waters. The ocean breeze was refreshing as they sat close, watching the waves and feeling the peace of being surrounded by God's creation.

The excitement was palpable as Troy and Love waded into the crystal-clear waters, guided by a team of experienced trainers. The sun glistened off the surface, creating a mesmerizing dance of light on the gentle waves. Just as they reached waist-deep water, a pod of sleek, playful dolphins glided toward them, their dorsal fins slicing effortlessly through the surface.

Love's eyes widened with childlike wonder as one of the dolphins swam right up to her, its smooth, gray body gleaming in the sunlight. She hesitated for just a moment before extending her hand, and to her delight, the dolphin gave her a gentle nudge. A burst of joyful laughter escaped her lips, the sound so pure and full of excitement that it made Troy chuckle.

"You see that?" Troy said, watching as another dolphin playfully circled around him before flipping onto its back, exposing its belly in an invitation for a rub. "I think we made some new friends."

The trainer smiled as he instructed them on how to interact with the dolphins. Following his guidance, Love held out her hand flat, and one of the dolphins responded by pressing its snout into her palm, as if giving her a little kiss. "Oh my goodness, Troy! Did you see that?" she exclaimed, beaming.

Troy grinned, watching the sheer happiness on his wife's face. "Yeah, I saw it. Guess they like you."

"Well, what's not to like?" she teased, winking at him.

As the session continued, they had the chance to experience a "dolphin ride," where Love held onto a dolphin's dorsal fin as it gracefully pulled her through the water. The rush of gliding effortlessly across the waves was exhilarating. Troy followed suit, his deep laughter echoing across the water as the dolphin propelled him forward with surprising speed.

Before the experience ended, the trainer guided them to a shallow spot where they could stand while the dolphins performed tricks—leaping high into the air, spinning, and even waving their fins in what looked like a cheerful farewell.

As they stepped out of the water, dripping and breathless from excitement, Love turned to Troy, eyes sparkling. "That was one of the most incredible experiences of my life."

He wrapped an arm around her, pulling her close. "Yeah? I think my favorite part was watching you laugh like that. It was beautiful."

She leaned into him, her heart overflowing with love and gratitude. "This whole trip has been magical. But moments like this... they make it unforgettable."

With one last glance back at the dolphins, who seemed to be watching them as well, the couple walked hand in hand toward the shore, their hearts full and their spirits lifted by the incredible connection they had just shared with the ocean's most playful creatures.

Their desire to embrace the island's culture led them to a small, welcoming village nestled among lush palm trees and vibrant tropical flowers. The moment they arrived, they were greeted with warm smiles from the locals, who adorned them with handmade floral leis as a symbol of friendship and hospitality. The air was filled with the rhythmic beat of island drums, and the scent of freshly prepared food wafted through the breeze.

They were led to an open clearing where a group of dancers performed a traditional island dance, their movements fluid and full of grace. Love and Troy watched in awe as the dancers told stories through their steps, their brightly colored skirts and intricate beadwork swaying with each motion. Soon, the villagers encouraged them to join in, and after a moment of hesitation, Love laughed and stepped forward, pulling Troy with her.

The instructor demonstrated the basic steps, and though they fumbled at first, they quickly caught on. Love giggled as Troy struggled to keep up, his two left feet making the villagers chuckle in amusement. "You're doing great, babe!" she teased, swaying her hips in rhythm with the music.

"Easy for you to say," he replied, grinning as he tried to mirror her movements.

After the dance, they moved on to a hands-on cooking class, where they learned how to prepare a beloved island dish. A kind elderly woman, who had been cooking for the village for decades, guided them through each step. She showed them how to grind fresh coconut to extract the milk and how to blend aromatic island spices to create the perfect marinade for their seafood dish.

Troy and Love worked side by side, laughing as they attempted to chop vegetables and stir the pot like seasoned chefs. At one point, Love accidentally spilled a bit of coconut milk on Troy, making him gasp dramatically.

"Now you've done it," he said, a mischievous glint in his eyes.

Before she could react, he playfully flicked a drop of sauce at her. The villagers around them erupted in laughter, enjoying the couple's lightheartedness.

Once the meal was ready, they sat down with their new friends to enjoy the feast. The flavors were rich and delicious, a true testament to the love and care that went into preparing each dish. Love sighed happily, savoring every bite. "I think we just found our new favorite meal," she said, nudging Troy.

"Agreed. But I think I'll leave the cooking to you," he joked, earning a playful nudge from her.

After their meal, they wandered through the village's artisan market, admiring the intricate craftsmanship of the local artists. Stalls were filled with handwoven baskets, delicate seashell jewelry, and stunning wood carvings. Love's eyes landed on a beautifully hand-carved wooden cross, its smooth edges polished to perfection. She ran her fingers over it, feeling a deep sense of peace.

Troy, meanwhile, was drawn to a painting of the ocean at sunrise, its colors capturing the breathtaking view they had admired each morning. He held it up, glancing at Love. "This reminds me of us—of God's faithfulness and the beauty of new beginnings," he said.

She smiled, her heart swelling with love. "Then it's perfect."

With their new treasures in hand, they thanked the villagers for their kindness and hospitality before making their way back to their resort. As they left, Love and Troy felt a profound sense of gratitude—not just for the experiences they had shared, but for the deeper connection they had formed, both with each other and with the culture that had welcomed them so warmly.

As the sun dipped below the horizon, the island came alive with the rhythmic beat of drums and the flickering glow of torches. Troy and Love made their way to the heart of the beach, where the cultural festival was in full swing. The air buzzed with excitement as locals and visitors gathered around a massive bonfire, its golden flames reaching toward the sky, casting dancing shadows on the sand.

They watched in awe as fire dancers moved effortlessly through the night, twirling flaming batons and spinning rings of fire with breathtaking precision. Each movement told a story—of strength, passion, and tradition—woven into the performance with mesmerizing grace. Drummers played in unison, their beats pulsing through the ground beneath their feet, making Love's heart race with excitement.

As the performances continued, the islanders invited guests to join in the festivities. Love and Troy, never ones to shy away from new experiences, stepped forward. A young woman wrapped a colorful sash around Love's waist, encouraging her to move with the rhythm of the drums. Troy, hesitant at first, gave in when an elder playfully handed him a small drum to join the beat. They laughed as they embraced the moment, swaying to the music, clapping, and celebrating the beauty of the culture surrounding them.

After the festivities wound down, Troy and Love strolled back to their villa, hand in hand, their hearts full from the incredible night. The warm ocean breeze carried the distant hum of music, mingling with the gentle sound of waves kissing the shore.

Back at their villa, they weren't quite ready to end the night. Instead, they stepped onto the deck, letting the cool night air wash over them as they settled onto a cozy lounge chair beneath the vast sky. The stars above were endless, scattered across the heavens like diamonds, a reminder of God's infinite greatness.

Troy reached for Love's hand and gently intertwined their fingers. "What a night," he said softly.

Love smiled, leaning into him. "It was incredible. I feel like every day here is a reminder of God's beauty—not just in the places we see, but in the people we meet and the moments we share."

With that thought, Love started humming a familiar melody, and soon, they were both singing their favorite worship songs together. Their voices blended in perfect harmony, their praises rising into the night, an offering of gratitude for all that they had been blessed with.

Between each song, they reflected on the goodness of God—on how far they had come as individuals and as a couple, and how every moment of their journey had been woven together by His divine plan.

Troy kissed Love's forehead and whispered, "I couldn't have asked for a better way to end this day."

Love looked up at him, her eyes shining with emotion. "Me neither. God is so good."

As they sat wrapped in each other's embrace, singing under the canopy of stars, they felt a peace that could only come from knowing they were exactly where they were meant to be.

CHAPTER 14

Day Trip to SRI LANKA
Day 5

On the fifth day, they were eager to explore beyond the Maldives, and what better way than a quick day trip to the stunning island of Sri Lanka? Excited for the adventure ahead, they woke up before sunrise, prayed together, and prepared for their journey. As always, they played a song while getting ready this one being *Total Praise* by Travis Malloy, setting the perfect tone for another blessed day.

Before stepping out, they stood at the villa door, held hands, and declared their daily scripture:

"Everywhere our feet walk today, God will be with us and give us victory." (Deuteronomy 11:24)

With that, they set off for the airport, boarding a short flight from Malé, Maldives, to Colombo, Sri Lanka, a breathtaking 90-minute journey over the endless blue ocean.

The moment they landed in Colombo, they were immediately enveloped by the vibrant energy of Sri Lanka. The city buzzed with life, a beautiful blend of rich culture, warm hospitality, and dynamic streets. Their first stop was the bustling Pettah Market, a lively maze of colorful stalls and friendly vendors eager to share their goods. The market overflowed with an array of treasures—vibrant fabrics, handcrafted jewelry, stylish footwear, intricate kitchenware, and an abundance of fresh produce. Love's eyes lit up with excitement as she eagerly explored the stalls, drawn to the unique finds and the rich diversity of offerings surrounding her.

Next, they ventured to the Pinnawala Elephant Orphanage, a sanctuary for rescued elephants. Watching the gentle giants bathe in the river and playfully spray water brought wide smiles to their faces. Love reached out to touch one of the elephants, feeling its rough yet warm skin beneath her fingertips. Troy snapped photos, capturing the joy on her face.

For lunch, they indulged in an authentic Sri Lankan meal at a local restaurant, savoring flavorful rice and curry, coconut sambal, and freshly baked roti. They laughed as they tried to eat the traditional way—with their hands—embracing every bit of the experience.

After lunch, they embarked on a breathtaking drive to Kandy, a city nestled in Sri Lanka's lush highlands. The rolling green hills and tea plantations stretched endlessly, making the ride feel like something out of a storybook.

At a local tea estate, they learned about the world-famous Ceylon tea and even participated in a traditional tea tasting session. As they sipped the perfectly brewed tea, Love leaned into Troy, appreciating the peacefulness of the moment.

"Can you believe we're here, in the middle of Sri Lanka, drinking tea on a mountaintop?" she whispered.

Troy chuckled. "I can believe it because with you, every adventure is possible."

As the sun dipped lower in the sky, they made their way back to the airport in Colombo, catching their evening flight back to the Maldives. From the window seat, they watched the golden hues of the sunset paint the ocean below, reflecting on how incredibly blessed they were to experience such a journey together.

Touching down in Malé, they felt a sense of homecoming as they returned to their private villa. The familiar warmth of the Maldivian air embraced them as they walked back into their luxurious retreat. Troy stepped aside, allowing Love to walk into the room first. Her eyes immediately landed on a beautifully wrapped bag resting on the bed with her name elegantly written on it. She turned to Troy, her eyes twinkling with curiosity.

"How did you...? What did you...?" she trailed off, excitement bubbling inside her as she reached for the bag.

Inside, she found a small velvet box. With eager hands, she opened it to reveal three new charms for her bracelet—a yacht, an ocean wave, and a camera.

"Troy," she breathed, her heart swelling with emotion.

"I wanted you to have something to remember this part of our trip," he said with a smile. "Every adventure we take together deserves a memory."

Love grinned as she held out her wrist. Troy carefully unclasped her bracelet, adding the new charms before fastening it back in place. She ran her fingers over each tiny symbol of their journey, feeling the weight of love and thoughtfulness behind every gift.

"You are full of surprises," she said, wrapping her arms around him.

"Troy bent down placing a gentle kiss on her forehead.

Though they had been away for the day, the villa still felt like a sanctuary—one filled with love, faith, and the unshakable presence of God.

To unwind from their travels, they took a moonlit swim in their private infinity pool, the water cool against their skin as they floated beneath a sky full of stars. Troy pulled Love close, placing a soft kiss on her lips.

"Today was incredible," Love whispered.

"And tomorrow will be even better," Troy replied, holding her hand as they gazed up at the heavens.

With grateful hearts, they ended the night the way they always did praying together, thanking God for another unforgettable day, and falling asleep wrapped in each other's arms.

CHAPTER 15

Day 6

On day six, even though every day felt like a blessing. They woke up before the sun in the reality of being with the person God had chosen just for them. Before anything else, they began their day in prayer, thanking God for His presence, His guidance, and the wonders He revealed to them daily. Hand in hand, they lifted their voices in worship, cherishing the sacred moments spent in devotion and study together.

As they prepared for their daily adventures, their villa was filled with the uplifting sound of music and praise. They sang along to their favorite worship song, "I'm So Blessed" by CAIN, allowing the powerful lyrics to wash over them like a sweet blessing. The melody set the perfect tone for the day, reminding them that they were truly blessed and that with God at the center of everything, all blessings flowed abundantly.

Though their last day on the island had come too quickly, they were determined to make every moment count. Stepping out onto the deck, they were greeted by the photographer who had just arrived for their sunrise and underwater photo shoot. Their excitement was palpable, eager for this unique experience that would capture their love and the beauty of the island in a way they'd never forget.

As the photographer set up his equipment, Love and Troy exchanged excited glances, their hearts racing with anticipation. The sun was still low in the sky, casting a soft golden glow over the ocean, the perfect light for their photos.

Hand in hand, they walked to the shoreline, the cool morning breeze ruffling through their hair as the waves gently lapping at their feet. The photographer directed them with a calm yet enthusiastic energy, capturing moments of laughter, quiet glances, and tender touches.

For the underwater portion of the shoot, they waded into the crystal-clear water, the photographer guiding them to a spot where the sun's rays pierced through the surface, creating a magical, shimmering effect. As they submerged into the cool embrace of the ocean, Love and Troy shared a quiet moment, holding each other close as they floated, the world around them fading away. The beauty of the ocean, the serenity of the moment, and the deep connection they shared were captured in perfect harmony.

Once the photo shoot wrapped up, they made their way back to the villa, laughing and playfully splashing each other with water as they exited the ocean. The photographer confirmed Troy's email address and assured him that the edited photos would be sent over soon. Troy shook his hand in appreciation, and they parted ways.

Troy then walked up to the deck, where Love was lounging in a chair. "Did you enjoy yourself?" he asked with a smile.

"Yes, I did! That was amazing," Love replied, her face lighting up with a huge grin.

"I'm so glad," Troy said, laying back in the chair, closing his eyes, and smiling contentedly.

Love stretched out beside him, gazing at the smile on the man she loved. In that moment, she silently thanked God for bringing him into her life and for the beautiful love they shared.

"Mr. Hayes," another young man called out as he walked up the steps to their deck.

"Yes?" Troy replied, sitting up.

"Are you and your beautiful wife ready for your cruise and snorkeling adventure?" the man asked.

Troy looked at Love and smiled. He stood, holding his hand out to her. "You ready, baby?"

"I'm always ready," she said with a grin.

He chuckled. "Well, we know if you stay ready, you don't have to get ready."

"Right," she replied, standing and taking his hand, following the young man.

"I'm Chad," the man introduced himself as they approached the boat, shaking their hands. "And this is my wife, Christine. She'll be taking pictures of you both during this excursion. We'll get your email and send the photos over to you afterward."

They spent a few hours cruising around several islands, diving and snorkeling to explore the vibrant underwater world. Chad navigated the boat from island to island while Christine captured the moments with her camera as they dove, swam, and floated. They marveled at the beauty of the ocean, the warmth of the sun on their skin, and the cool embrace of the water as they enjoyed the serenity of the moment and the incredible marine life beneath the surface.

As their excursion came to an end, Chad steered the boat back toward the shore. Love and Troy, both relaxed and content from their underwater adventures, sat side by side, watching the tranquil waters and reflecting on the incredible experiences of the day.

Christine, who had been snapping photos throughout the trip, gathered her camera equipment and smiled at them. "I've got so many great shots! I'll send them to you as soon as possible."

Troy smiled and nodded, his arm around Love's shoulders. "We can't wait to see them. Thank you!" It was a moment they knew they would forever hold in their hearts, knowing the memories they created would last a lifetime.

Once back on the dock, they thanked Chad and Christine for the unforgettable experience. It was about noon as they made their way back to their villa, hand in hand, silently grateful for the beauty of the activities so far and the bond they shared. As they entered their villa, they decided to unwind with a quiet lunch on the deck, basking in the glow of the sun. After lunch they decided to wash off the sea and spend the day relaxing with each other.

That evening, as they sat on the beach, watching the sunset, Love turned to Troy with a thoughtful look. "Troy, this has been incredible—so many blessings, so much joy. But I know that we're just beginning to build our future together and it seems as if we have been together for a lifetime. What are your hopes for us? What do you see for us in the future?"

Troy took her hand, looking out at the horizon. "I see a lifetime of love, of adventures, of building a family. I see us growing together in faith, supporting each other through the highs and lows. I see us becoming the couple God always intended us to be strong, loving, unified, the couple others see showing the pure love of God and strength together."

Tears welled up in Love's eyes as she gazed at him, her heart brimming with gratitude. "I see the same," she said softly. "And with God at the center of our marriage, I know we'll be unstoppable."

Troy nodded, his voice firm with conviction. "We'll never give up on us, no matter what challenges Satan tries to throw our way. He doesn't want any marriage to succeed, but with God, all things are possible. Our marriage will stand the test of time."

Love smiled through her tears, her voice steady with unwavering faith. "We will not fail."

They leaned in and kissed, their hearts brimming with promise for the future.

"Excuse me, Mr. and Mrs. Hayes," their butler, Les, said, gently interrupting. "Sorry to disturb you. I just wanted to check if you'd prefer dinner in your villa tonight or here on the beach.

"Yes, we'll have dinner here at the villa," Troy said.

"Very good, sir," Les responded, bowing slightly before turning to leave.

"Les?" Troy called, stopping him.

Les turned around. "Yes, Mr. Hayes?"

"Are we set up to go to the airport in the morning?" Troy asked.

"Yes, Mr. Hayes everything is set for your travels to the airport" Les responded.

"Awesome!" Troy responded.

Moments later, Les and the other servers brought over their final dinner of the evening. They savored a delicious Seafood Paella, complete with lobster and shrimp, paired with refreshing coconut water.

After their final dinner, Love and Troy spent some quiet time packing, the weight of their impending departure beginning to settle in. They moved slowly through their villa, folding clothes and gathering their belongings, reluctant to leave the paradise they had grown to love.

As the last of their items were packed, they sat together on the edge of the bed, both feeling a mix of gratitude and sadness for the beautiful time they had shared.

"I don't want this to end," Love whispered, her voice soft with emotion.

Troy smiled gently, holding her tighter. "Baby, we have so many more adventures ahead."

With the soft glow of the room surrounding them, Troy gently pulled Love closer, their bodies naturally aligning as they shared a tender, lingering kiss. In that intimate moment, their whispered words of love and appreciation filled the space, the quiet connection between them speaking louder than any words could express. Each touch, each glance, each beat of their hearts was a silent testament to the bond they had grown over the past few days.

They slipped under the sheets together, the warmth of their bodies creating a peaceful stillness in the air. For a while, they simply lay there, talking in soft tones, their voices barely above a whisper as they shared promises of love and dreams of the future. The intimacy between them deepened as their kisses grew more passionate, but it was about more than just the physical connection—it was a bond that transcended the surface, an emotional depth that stirred something far greater within both of them. They were intertwined not just in body, but in soul, in a way that went beyond words, touching places inside each of them that only the other could reach.

Eventually, they fell asleep, wrapped in each other's arms, their hearts beating in perfect sync.

CHAPTER 16

The next morning arrived far too quickly, their alarms went off at 4 a.m., pulling them from their restful sleep. They moved quietly, gathering their things one last time. With bright eyes and prayerful hearts, they made their way to the airport, hearts full but heavy as they headed to their 5 a.m. flight back to the U.S. not quite ready to say goodbye to the paradise they'd just begun to fully appreciate.

As they sat in the airport, hand in hand, Troy squeezed Love's hand, a silent promise that no matter where their travels took them, they would always have each other. Once more with closed eyes Troy prayed "Lord guide the pilot and this airplane keep up in the air no matter what today God you will be with us and give us victory." And though the island was behind them, the memories and the love they had shared would stay with them forever.

Their flight from the Maldives to Charleston, South Carolina, was long, filled with a combination of excitement and bittersweetness. They boarded the international flight, settled into their seats with anticipation. The hum of the aircraft and the gentle motion of the plane provided a sense of comfort as they made their way across the world.

As the plane ascended, Love rested her head on Troy's shoulder. He gently brushed a loc from her face, his hand lingering against her cheek. They exchanged quiet smiles, both reflecting on their time together. Though the Maldives had been an enchanting escape, they knew their real adventure was just beginning—together. The sun began to rise, casting soft hues of pink and gold across the sky as they sat on the flight that spanned multiple time zones, and though they'd been on the move for hours, there was a peaceful rhythm to the journey. They spent time in the quiet hum of the cabin, occasionally drifting off into light sleep, waking up to find each other's hands still intertwined. Meals were served, and the long hours passed in a blur of comfort, laughter, and small moments of connection. They spoke more about their future and the dreams they hoped to achieve, the life they wanted to build together.

The flight included two stops, first in Dubai where they ate a late lunch and then in Miami here, they enjoyed a quiet breakfast. The stops gave them a chance to stretch their legs and refresh, but by the time they arrived in Miami they were exhausted but also felt a sense of anticipation building. As the last two hours of plane ride made its final descent into Charleston, the air grew thicker with humidity, a familiar warmth that welcomed them home. "Last but not least," Troy said with a grin, handing Love yet another small box.

She couldn't help but laugh, shaking her head at his endless surprises. "Troy, you are something else," she teased, but her excitement was undeniable.

She carefully opened the box, her eyes widening as she found three more charms nestled inside—two intertwined hearts, an 'I DO' charm, and one that read 'FOREVER US.'

Her heart melted as she held them in her palm. "Troy..." she whispered, overwhelmed by his thoughtfulness.

Without a word, she held out her wrist, and he gently unclasped the bracelet, adding the new charms with the same care he had shown each time before. Once fastened back in place, she ran her fingers over the tiny tokens of their love, her smile radiant.

"I never want to take it off," she said softly, gazing up at him with pure adoration.

Troy kissed her hand, his eyes filled with love. "You'll never have to, baby."

As the aircraft began its descent, Love leaned against Troy's shoulder, her heart full, knowing their love story and how amazing it has began.

As the plan glided towards the runway, the familiar sights of Charleston came into view. The city, with its charm and southern hospitality, felt like a stark contrast to the tropical paradise they had left behind, but it was home. They gathered their bags and walked off the plane, hand in hand, feeling the comfort of returning to familiar ground.

Walking through the airport, they shared a quiet excitement about returning to their everyday lives but also knowing that the bond they had forged during their time in Paris, Dubai, Maldives and Sri Lanka would stay with them forever. As they headed to the exit, they couldn't help but reflect on how their love had grown so deeply over the past two weeks, and though their international trips had been beautiful, their journey was only just beginning. They had a lifetime of memories to create starting with their arrival back in Charleston. As they stepped out of the doors of the airport, they could hear the hustle and bustle of daily life but a Sunday calm. They smiled at each other; Troy squeezed her hand and then began the walk towards the driver waiting on them. Back home, beginning their beautiful life together. With flutters in her stomach Love smiled as she walked hand in hand with her Husband and God by her side.

ABOUT THE AUTHOR

Blue Kendria Berry is a proud native of Columbia, SC, whose journey has taken her across many places, thanks to her family's deep-rooted military background. A devoted child of Yahweh, she carries a profound passion for His people and the art of storytelling.

Her professional career spans both the legal field and customer service, where her commitment to excellence has always been evident. However, her love for writing began much earlier—back in the 5th grade—when she penned her first book of short stories. Over the years, she continued crafting multiple stories and novellas, eventually writing her first novel in 2010. In 2023, she embarked on this novella, a labor of faith and inspiration, which she proudly completed in December 2024 and published in January 2025.

Beyond writing, Blue is a dynamic entrepreneur. She is the owner of **Blue's Notary Services** and **Beautiful Kreations**, a thriving skincare brand specializing in handcrafted body scrubs and body butters. Her creativity and determination shine through in every endeavor she pursues.

Above all, Blue is a devoted mother to an extraordinary daughter who has followed in her footsteps as both an author and entrepreneur, continuing a legacy of creativity and resilience. Stay tuned for more inspiring works from Blue Kendria Berry in the near future!

Find additional resources and information about
Blue Kendria Berry at
Website - www.beautifulkreations.shop
Facebook - @Blue Kendria
Tiktok - @Blue_Kendria
Instagram - @beautifulkreationsllc

www.ingramcontent.com/pod-product-compliance
Lightning Source LLC
LaVergne TN
LVHW072050060526
838201LV00029B/323/J